BELIEVE

BELIEVE

A journey of hope

Roy Chester

AMHERST

ISBN 1 903637 21 X

Printed in Great Britain

First published in 2004 by

Amherst Publishing Limited
Longmore House, High Street, Otford, Sevenoaks, Kent TN14 5PQ

For my family

Chapter One

Strawberries

RED, ripe, and firm; their sweet smell hangs just under your nose, almost hinting at the taste. Jumping out of the car, and seeing row upon row of strawberries, I knew I couldn't pick all of them, and invariably more would end up in my mouth than in the basket. To a four-year-old, it must have seemed that even Hercules would find this task impossible.

Grabbing Ian's hand, I couldn't wait to start picking, but adults never do things the way children would. My impatience would build up into a ball of butterflies in my tummy, just waiting to explode until I was handed a small basket to carry my berry treasure. Filling the basket is a daunting task. Not only did each strawberry demand to be tasted as soon as it was picked, but the first one in the basket always seemed so lonely. Ian would follow two steps behind, carefully watching his older brother and then trying to do what I did.

With the first strawberry fatality staining Ian's little hand, the juice dripping onto the ground from his palm. His eyes, almost tearful would look into mine, and I would pick one for him and let him eat it.

'Don't squish it,' I would tell him sternly. Guiltily he would look into his empty basket and I would pick a couple more to get him on his way. I think Ian looked up to me, and I was certainly proud of how quickly he made up for the age difference.

We were happy. Every day brought about a new adventure, and there was always something new to learn. Life was exciting, nothing felt like a chore. But I was not much more than a toddler, and it's very sad that children grow out of that passionate excitement for life faster than they do their clothes.

I can remember our holidays quite clearly. We would spend hours and hours in the car, and just when I thought I couldn't sit any longer, my dad would stop the car. I'm sure everyone suffers from the frustrating 'are we there yet?' syndrome, both the kids asking, well, usually demanding, and the parents listening. The first officially recorded case of passenger rage was Henry Ford's oldest. But if anyone took the time to check, they would probably find out that little Romans in the backs of chariots would pull on their father's toga, and ask, 'advenio illic sumus, pater?'

Of course, Ian and I didn't just annoy our parents with our constant questions and chatter. Sometimes we would annoy each other as well. At that time it was assumed it was safe to be a passenger, and we were still several years away from compulsory seatbelts, which meant, whenever the mood took us, we would fight.

And these were proper tantrum-fuelled toddler fights that would put the American Wrestling Federation to shame. Ian is eighteen months younger than me, but he gave as good as he got. People assume that because children don't have adult worries, their anger and frustrations are trivial. Worry is worry whatever it is about. But to a toddler who can't make himself understood, communication is yet another reason for anger and worry.

In those fleeting moments between me flying out of the car and finding out what would happen next, my imagination would fly into overdrive with all the possibilities. I don't think I ever lost that, because even now, whether I'm about to open a new book, or enter a fresh field with my metal detector, the spark that ignites the imagination is still there.

However sunny it got, it was never warm enough to go swimming in the sea, but letting the tide tickle your toes made the holiday more special. I was happy just chasing Ian around the sand dunes, or playing hide-and-seek. It didn't matter if it was raining, we could always find something to do. There were board games to hand, and often we would play guessing games, or even race raindrops from the inside of the windows. Staying in a caravan meant we would have to be inventive about use of space, but for Ian and myself that was just another part of play.

Of course, sunny days were much better. We could go exploring, never sure what we would find. From an early age, I acquired a love of fishing, and often Ian and I would sit on a log nearby, hands on knees, with bated breath expectant of something. Without even a blink, I watched intently, frightened I would miss the one movement that the act of fishing relied on for success. I soon learned the technicalities, but to this day I find it impossible to say exactly why it appeals. Is it relaxing? Is it calming? Does it give you the opportunity to ponder your life and others? Grab a rod and sit by the bank for a while.

We used to go camping as well. We had sleeping bags, but we didn't use groundsheets, Dad used to put bracken underneath us, and camping in England meant waking up colder than if you'd spent the night naked in a fridge, so we always had extra blankets, and they were always used. During the night I would get bitten by every insect in the county. They must have hated me with a vengeance; I can't imagine that there exists a flying bug I'm not allergic to. I itched and swelled, and more often than not I would feel faint. After pitching the tent, we would light a fire, which of course meant feeding time for the insects as well, and we would have our usual. The Chester family menu was, to say the least, predictable. The sort of food my mother prepared for us was what you could call popular rather than traditional. My mum was never very good with pots and pans, and I have a feeling that food was only a chore she kept up in order to stay alive. My dad was much the same in that more often than not he would leave that side of things to my mother.

So when we went on holiday it would normally mean takeaways - our favourite was fish and chips. Before takeaways became big business and opened up on every corner, it was quite common to see mobile catering trailers parked, serving food. Perhaps I only remember the portions being so big, because I was small; it often seemed I wouldn't be able to carry it, let alone eat it. So my dad would be there ready to help. Sometimes he took it all off me, if he thought I was going to drop it, but usually, all I would see was a finger and thumb in a pincer movement, heading towards my chips.

Every time we arrived in Blackpool, the first thing I wanted to see was the dancing monkey, though I wasn't too interested in the man playing the organ. And when we visited Margate, which wasn't often, we would visit a pub where they prepared special drinks for children, and they made it out of whatever fruit they had, apples and grapes usually. What made this pub really great, was the fact that next door there was a shop, which sold those big paper 'lucky bags', which had plenty of sweets, and some sort of toy, and sometimes a puzzle. Also they had a big wooden case, inside which there were puppet dogs singing, 'How much is that doggy in the window?'

I can remember one summer - we must have spent most of it at home - because I have vivid memories of watching John Hackett making us a go-cart. He used pram wheels, and a big box. Now John was Colin and Gary's dad, and we played together all the time. We got on really well. Colin was Ian's age, and Gary was the same age as me. We all thought John was quite a scary man, because he wore an earring. This must have been really unusual otherwise I would never have remembered it so clearly. I think up to that point I'd only ever seen pirates in storybooks with earrings. We raced from the moment we were allowed outside the front door to the moment we were called back in. No amount of blood, cuts, or bruises could stop us going up and down the street and back again. We even went away together, two families sharing a holiday, so the children would have company instead of being left to their own devices.

Back home in Keresley End, things were no different. I was in a safe environment, doing what all kids do – play, learn, make mistakes and try again. There was always so much to do in between playing. I guess for a while it all seemed like a game.

It seemed like the whole world was ours to explore, no-one stopped us from venturing further and further each time. We often played on the field behind our house when we were with our friends, because it seemed like such a huge space and it was all ours. We would be running around, using up energy doing nothing in particular. Sometimes I wonder how so much energy fits into such a little person!

We had a huge garden. It was a wonderful place to explore. Trudging through the grass, I could have been in any jungle in the world, sometimes fighting a war, sometimes on the brink of finding a lost city. The gate to all these lost cities was in fact the shed door. We didn't go into the shed very often. It was dark and full of shadows that didn't always have an owner as far as I could see.

Sometimes the shed would be a fort; on other days it was a prisoner of war camp. It would depend on what we had seen on television the previous day as to who the baddies were and why we were fighting them. I don't remember spending a lot of time sitting still. In fact I'm not sure where and when I did acquire that skill. Even watching TV didn't keep me in one place. Ian and I used to watch Bill and Ben. I think we laughed more at how they spoke, not so much at what they said, and with time we grew to understand it on different levels, until we grew out of it. Pinky and Perky was another show I remember distinctly. In fact Ian and I pestered our mum and dad until they filled in the forms so we could join their fan club. Every child in the neighbourhood seemed to be a member, and the club used to provide us with all sorts of gifts, including a record of the two stars singing.

I say singing, but if I played it now I think my eardrums would burst from the high pitched squeaks, and every dog within twenty miles would be howling at my door. At the time it was the best thing since sliced bacon. Just goes to show, children have such resilience.

On a wet day (we were in England after all), we would play inside, getting under our parents' feet, although, on the odd occasion that we did stay out in the rain, we would get soaked through. We didn't have waterproofs, and from what I can remember we spent a lot of time in woollen jumpers. Even so it was fun, especially jumping bang in the middle of a puddle, listening for the splash, but never hearing it, because there was always a surprised shriek to let you know the cold water had splashed a warm dry leg nearby.

Inside, we played hide and seek and we never tired of it, even though we only used three hiding places. My first choice would be in the wardrobe, but that was only until my association of safety of the familiar smells and warmth was forcibly taken away from me. Another favourite place to hide was under the bed. It was absolutely enormous, dark and foreboding. Later, as I got bigger, it became claustrophobic, but even that was better than what was waiting for me on the other side.

In our room, Ian and I had a massive iron double bed and a single bed to choose from. Climbing in would be like attempting Everest; it must have been at least two feet off the floor. We swapped often, never really minding where we woke up, because our mum would put us into her bed until we fell asleep, and then she would carry us back into our own room.

It was a nightly ritual, after our bath, to go into the living room and stand by the coal fire to dry. There was something special, almost magical, about those flames. They flickered invitingly, and as long as you were respectful, it gave warmth and light and comfort. We would get into our pyjamas, which had been hanging over the fire guard, so they were nice and warm, and we would go upstairs, sometimes willingly, and at other times kicking and screaming, but however we got to the first floor, we knew we could cuddle in Mum's and Dad's big bed.

Even though we had our own big bed, it was never the same thing. I suppose a parents' bed feels like you're snuggling into a great big hug of safety and love, while at the same time it is intriguing and mysterious, because we were never allowed to stay the whole night.

And as every parent knows, one story is never enough at bedtime, no matter how heavy the eyelids are. I'm not sure we ever got through a whole story without interrupting. Ian would ask why, and I would ask detailed questions that even the Grimm brothers could not have found immediate answers to. But as every child knows, the parents have all the answers, or so it seems.

In our room we had shelves in the alcoves, where we kept our toys and aeroplanes, although some of them used to hang from the ceiling. My favourite was a Spitfire, and as I also had a die-cast Messerschmitt, I was happy to play air raids and dog fights all day long. When I had the patience to sit down long enough, I would set up whole armies of toy soldiers and then shoot them with a cannon. This particular cannon used to fire matchsticks, and I was never any good at aiming. After trying to destroy the enemy for so long with normal warfare, I would give up on the cannon, and just trample them instead. The cannon was obviously not my weapon of choice, but later on, when given the opportunity to learn to handle a real weapon, I took to shooting and was what I suppose you could call a natural with an air rifle or a shotgun.

The house, as I remember it, was big, safe and interesting. I liked the living room best of all, because we used to be in there as a family. Even though I liked the television, my favourite thing was the fireplace. Apart from the kitchen that was brown, for some inexplicable reason, the rest of the house was the now infamous magnolia. Before the likes of TV designers taking over our walls and creating features for them, or out of them, most houses I knew seemed to be non-descript in colour. I suppose magnolia was popular because it was not white, and bland enough not to be offensive to anyone else.

It all may sound like an ordinary, boring childhood, but I loved it all the same. I am grateful that my memories from my past gave me hope and something to believe in for the future, because my present was soon to become a nightmare that all the adults around me chose to ignore.

Chapter Two

Meet the family

BORN on the 14th of May in 1965, I was the first child of David Conway Chester and Brenda. I was named after my father, but in order to save confusion, everyone called me by my middle name, Roy. I must have been a fairly good baby because I didn't put them off from having another. In fact, I didn't spend a lot of time by myself because, eighteen months later, Ian Andrew was introduced to me as my little brother.

When I was born, we were living with my Nan Hutchings, although throughout my childhood I would never be too far away because Keresley End was and still is so small. Before he started working in the pits, my father worked as a textile dyer for the same company my mother worked for. I get the impression, hearing them speak about it later, that working at Cashes was enjoyable. They never said it was easy work, but most people would get on, so that made the shift go by easily.

My mother must have been in her early thirties when she had me, and by all accounts, she was a friendly, sociable woman. No matter what else was happening, she would always make time for her friends. She was happiest when she was competing or gambling. She led the women's darts team, and still goes bowling even now. It must have been difficult to come to terms with giving up a night-life for a bundle of screams and smells, but I think she loved me then.

I can't think of a time when there wasn't a cigarette perched on Brenda's lower lip, the ash sometimes clinging on, drooping, but not quite breaking off until she gave it an indifferent flick. Brenda, even now, is never far away from her 'circle' - her friends were so important to her. She was inseparable from her pack of twenties. I never lost sight of her in a crowd because there always seemed to be cloud of smoke about six inches above her head.

My mother was very strict about bedtime, and no matter what else was happening, we had to be in bed by six, winter or summer, rain or shine, no exception. I can remember crying because all my friends would stop out playing, but Ian and I had to be in bed. It didn't seem fair. During the summer, I hoped the rag and bone man would come by before we had to go in, because he would arrive on his horse and cart, and ask us if we had anything for him. We used to make a special effort for him, because if we gave him anything he would give us a balloon, and if we got him a really big pile of clothes he would give us a goldfish.

It didn't matter to her particularly whether we were at home or on holiday, if there were a bingo game on, she would be playing. Brenda made good use of her contacts at the bingo hall, because it was one of her friends there who would lend us her caravan whenever we wanted to get away.

Brenda was and is a self-centred woman. Is this because she was the youngest of ten siblings, and got away with murder as a child? Or was it because by the time she settled to have children she was already too long in the life she enjoyed to want to give it up? She danced, she drank, she socialised, and did whatever she thought necessary to make her life more pleasant. No husband or child would get in the way.

I was very close to my father. I idolised him, and no toddler could have glowed with more pride for being his son. I assume every child is overwhelmed by the love they have for their parents, so I was no different. He was always considerate, to all of us, and no matter how hard he worked, he made time to listen to us and to be with us. He would try to make things interesting for us; whenever he brought something home, he would tie a piece of string or wool around it and leave a trail for us to follow. Usually it was only something small, but we loved the expectation just as much as the gift. Our hearts pumping faster and harder the more we tugged on the string. One evening, Ian and I were given a string each, and the further we moved along, the more excited we got, and the faster we searched. We both gasped, and it felt like I had jumped out of my skin with surprise when both our strings led to a rocking horse. It was brown and white, standing beautifully in the light of the coal fire. If we were good, we would be allowed to ride on it after we had dressed for bed.

David was a meticulous man who bred rabbits, and he showed them as much care as he would have shown a pet. It took me a long time to realise that so many of them were served up next to their favourite orange nibbles. His other hobby was fishing, which he introduced us to from an early age. It seems that every time he got the chance he would go sea-fishing, but I don't think he ever caught anything. He gave us small metal rods, with plastic reels, and bent two pins for us to use as hooks. He taught us how to find worms to use as bait. We caught lots of newts, sticklebacks and such, at the pond that was just down at the end of the road. This pond had a fallen tree in it, and we used to try and balance on it to get closer to the fish. Many a time I fell in, coming out drenched and smelling like the bottom of the pond. I spent a lot of time there, and in the fields around it.

I never had my own bike, but my dad would let me borrow his, when he thought I was big enough. It must be hard learning to ride when you're only a couple of inches off the ground, but I couldn't have been more than half my father's height when I enthusiastically jumped on… and flew over the other side. One bruised elbow later, I tried again, this time with a little support, and I made it! About 50 yards, that is. But even with all the cuts and bruises, I enjoyed riding that bike. My father never made me feel it was a bad thing that I was a little boy with so much growing up to do. He made the effort to treat me like a little person, rather than an adult not yet formed.

The only other person who showed me the same sort of respect, and treated me as a person, was Nan Hutchings, my mother's mother. How that woman could have produced a child that grew up into the woman who gave birth to me, I'll never understand. Perhaps age brings its own patience, maybe having ten of her own made it easier for her to be with somebody else's child.

I could never say she spoiled me, but whenever I was in her company, she made the time to talk to me, and to play. I seem to remember spending a lot of time with her. It was a long trek to her house, or at least it seemed like it to my little legs. I was forever scurrying, trying to keep up, but in reality she lived close by. We stopped with her quite often because both Mum and Dad were working nights.

She would sing us nursery rhymes; I liked the ones with actions best of all. Just before bedtime, she would place a piece of cheese into the Aga, which dominated the living room. It was almost as if it had an air of superiority over other household appliances, its rightful place nowhere near the kitchen. She would allow the cheese to melt so it was soft and gooey in time for the fresh baked bread. We would get a glass of warm milk to go with our supper. I loved to watch her kneading the dough, because it usually meant that while we waited for it to rest and double in size, we would play some sort of game. Even when she was busy I felt wanted in her company.

Nan Chester had a junior penny-farthing, and although it was the right sort of size, it didn't seem much easier than my dad's bike. With practice, I was soon riding around with ease and stopping with the brakes rather than my chin. She lived in Holbrook, about five miles away, and although I don't remember it that way, we must have gone quite often, because I remember being told Nan, Granddad, Mum and Dad used to go to Bingo together. I never met my maternal grandfather; I have a feeling my mother was pregnant with me when he died. For some reason, and no-one in the family can work out why, my maternal grandparents used different versions of the surname. Nan was Hutchings, but granddad used Hutching. So I have no idea which is correct, because even on the gravestone, both are used.

Once granddad Chester had died, and Nan had got over the shock, she packed everything away and left for Spain. I must have been in my teens by then, because I can remember it quite clearly. One of her other sons, the one that wasn't mentioned in polite conversation because he was gay, was already out there, successfully running his own night clubs on the coast. She couldn't have been gone for more than three months, when we found out that she also had died. I think she didn't want to live without her husband, and just gave up on life.

In Nan Chester's garden, she had an apple tree and a blackcurrant bush, and however good the fruit tasted fresh from the garden, Nan would always manage to do something even better with it in her kitchen. Nan Hutchings also was a cook of the old school. If we happened to be around, she wouldn't be at all frightened about giving us a running commentary about what she was doing. She believed in teaching by example, and she saw no harm in me learning something I might find useful later on. Whether it was cooking, or knitting and sewing, Nan made sure I was competent before starting something else.

We would spend Christmas at my Nan Chester's. The house would be full of aunts and uncles, and there would always be someone at the piano singing. Room would be made for dancing, and it always seemed like a happy but exhausting time.

My granddad Chester was also a splendid man. A large man, but softly spoken, we knew we could always find him in the garden, and when he thought we were old enough, we would help him as much as we could. He taught me so many things that would be of use to me throughout my life, from making the most of a garden, to all the odd jobs that need doing around the house. He wasn't so bad when it came to the car either.

An uncle of mine had a farm, and sometimes when we stopped with Nan and Granddad Chester, they would take us to visit him. We loved riding on the tractor, and if we had been really good, they would take us to see the steam trains, or to a tea room. Granddad had a soft spot when it came to kids and sweets. I suppose now it must have been a bit of a game. He would hide the sweets and give them to us when Nan wasn't looking. Whenever she caught us out she would go mad, saying there's no fool like an old fool, and we were only rotting our teeth.

I remember I was near the Aga at Nan Hutchings' house when I noticed a movement across the floor. It was as if something was slithering from one shadow to another. I pointed it out to my Nan, who, without any sign that I should be worried, got up to get her axe. I sat there waiting to see what would happen next. She came back, axe in hand, and waited. The snake came into view, and two, three swings of the axe later, it lay by her feet, in shreds. We didn't find out until later that it was an adder, so we were lucky she acted so fast. Once it was cleaned away I knew I had been scared, but Nan was so efficient in dealing with it that I felt safe, and I knew she would always protect me. After the adder slaying, Nan was a bit of a hero in my eyes. It was almost as if I could hear the bugle announcing her presence just as I had seen in the comic books. Da da da... snake slayer to the rescue!

Even when I knew that there was no going back, and that I had no choice but to leave my dad and live with Brenda and Bob, Nan Hutchings stepped in as she had so many times before when Brenda had fought with David. She agreed to take me in while Bob got my room ready. This transition was made a little easier because I spent some time with Nan, but it didn't dull the pain of separation and change.

Nan had been a seamstress by trade, and she would take work, a lot of work, home with her. Others would come by and ask if she could do them a favour. Invariably these people all wanted clothes taken up. For some reason the manufacturers all seemed to think the people of Keresley had longer arms and legs than we actually did. Or maybe our limbs are shorter than average. Whenever I asked, Nan would tell me she was shortening something.

It all started with Mum getting pregnant for the third time. She must have stopped work, which would have meant there would be less money and more mouths to feed. We started to take in lodgers; Ian and I preferred to share a room, so there was one spare. Dad was working all the hours possible, both at work, and with the rabbits, so I think he was too tired not to go along with it.

Most of the lodgers were quite nice, but with time, my memories of them have more or less blended into one another. One in particular stands out, because at the time, it was unusual to see Europeans, never mind blacks. Vernon was always nice to Ian and me. He brought with him some wonderful African carvings which I was content just to stare at. I'm sure he told me all about them and what they represented, because I do not believe I would have been able to go days, let alone months, without asking what they were. He also had a small set of drums which he played for us, and sometimes he would let us have a go. He also had the patience to try to teach me to play the guitar. I'm not too sure what other people in Keresley End thought of us for having such an exotic guest, but for me it was exciting to meet someone from a different culture. Even now, I'm not sure how many foreigners have integrated.

I don't think Mum cooked for Vernon; perhaps his own cuisine was preferable to the traditional west Midlands fare. It must have been the case, because she would go out of an evening and call a babysitter to stop with us. I remember this very well, because during an argument my parents had with Vernon, I heard him mention Ison's name. I have no idea what it was about, but soon after, Vernon moved away.

Because I missed Vernon, I asked my parents why he had moved away, and they told me that he was sick of all the arguing going on in our house, so he thought it best if he left.

Some of the others who stayed with us, also wanted meals. I was happy about this, because if nothing else, it meant Mum would stay at home, even if she was busy. Yet whenever Brenda had the opportunity, she would go out; sometimes we spent night after night with babysitters because she wanted time to herself. While we were small enough, and she could put us to bed at six o'clock, we were none the wiser what she did once we were asleep. As we managed with less sleep, I became acutely aware of the feeling of being abandoned. It was a natural reaction to miss the one closest to you.

The money situation obviously was not improving by much, because once Brenda had recovered from the birth of Lucy in October 1970, she found herself another job. It seems to me that even with the extra money she was getting she wasn't able to manage the house and her night-life. Things must have been difficult, because there were arguments all the time, and each one seemed louder and more vicious than the last. Memories are subjective, and perhaps I'm remembering my fear and ignorance as well as watching or hearing these arguments, but I had no signs that my fears were unfounded. Brenda started going out whenever she could, day or night, but she did try to get her mother to look after us while she argued with our father. While Dad was at work, and Mum saw a chance to escape from the house, she would call a babysitter. During this time she started cleaning houses, and she started working for Bob.

Where my Mum would escape, Dad would bring his friends home, and this annoyed Brenda something silly. When she was itching for a fight she would mention one of Dad's friends, and of course he would get defensive, so sometimes within seconds an argument would erupt. If he had gone out, he was easy to find; there was just the one pub in our village. But even so, Mum would make a big deal of it, getting us all dressed and ready to go out looking for him.

This pub, The Golden Eagle, served the whole of Keresley End exclusively. The village had about three thousand inhabitants, most of them making up the local manual labour force. Most of them would have also called themselves regulars. So no-one could go in there and say how hard it was working in the pit and expect sympathy when more or less every other face in there was tinged with coal dust. The Golden Eagle was always full, and the noise used to spill out, as did the drinkers. Fights were common, which should have been expected, but people didn't bear grudges – not particularly because they were considerate, but mostly because a fight is not worth becoming a teetotaller for.

I can remember one Saturday afternoon, Dad had taken us to the pub, well to the car park actually, and we waited for him while he got us our usual - a drink of pop and a packet of crisps. Back inside, Dad was with his own mates, and Ian and I stayed in the car park playing. Dad got himself into a fight - all around him shards of glass lay on the floor. We wouldn't have known anything about it, but someone had broken a window. Amongst the usual pub noise, that distinct and recognisable thwack of knuckle against cheek could be heard. Ian and I started crying, perhaps to drown out the noise, but mostly because we had never seen such physical violence close to hand.

We got home, and Mum took one look at Dad; it was obvious he didn't manage to have that quiet drink he had been after. She glanced over at our tear-stained faces and decided there and then we could never go to the pub with Dad again.

Some nights my parents made the effort to be civil to each other, and sometimes they even got on well. When that happened they would usually go out for the evening, most probably to the bingo hall. They would come back with fish and chips still steaming in the paper. The TV was switched on, and I remember it being on as loud as it would go – especially if they'd had a drink. From upstairs I could hear the ten o'clock news. I recognised it by the Big Ben chimes at the beginning. I would sneak downstairs and wait for them to notice me. Dad would call me to sit by him, and sometimes he would even put me in his lap and give me chips. I loved that simple interaction between father and son; it was a comforting sign among all the others showing that my world was about to fall apart.

When they finally made the decision not to stay together, I was given the choice of who I wanted to be with. No-one bothered to ask Ian or Lucy; it was assumed that they would want to be with their mother. It turned out that I had no choice. The other two would be with Brenda, and I didn't want to choose between my brother and my father. Thinking about it later, I knew even if I had chosen to stay with David, it would have been more trouble than it was worth. He had to go to work, and there would be no-one to look after me. I didn't want to be alone without Ian to play with, and I certainly did not want to be left on my own with babysitters.

Ian, being the younger one, probably struggled even more than I did, trying to comprehend what was happening. Young children sense feelings and emotions in what is going on around them before they are old enough to understand the facts of a situation. So he would get very upset, very easily, and Mum would take him out with her. I used to get upset too, but maybe she thought I was old enough to cope. This just made me feel even more isolated, as Dad would have his own feelings to deal with, and he obviously preferred to deal with them on his own, rather than talk to a child about them.

One day she put Ian on her bike and they disappeared for hours. There was a knock at the door, and Dad and I thought they had returned, but it was a police officer, telling us that Mum and Ian had been knocked off the bike by a car. Both were covered in cuts and bruises, but all the injuries were superficial and healed quickly.

Brenda and David made a special effort after that, and they got on for a while; we even went away on a camping holiday. I would love to know who informs the flying bugs that I'm on holiday (they must be on commission). Surely they lie in wait, and as soon as they see me they go berserk and ambush me.

There was one occasion where I got my own back on the little blighter. Mum had left us with a babysitter. Brenda didn't even wait for us to finish bathing. The babysitter took us out of the bath, and I sat down without looking, waiting for her to pass me my pyjamas. I never expected to sit on a bee, which proved even in death it can still sting. And it hurt like hell. I had a bad reaction, and to this day I still hate all flying bugs that seem to have it in for me.

Mum carried on working, and about this time she must have started her affair with Bob. Like my father, he worked in the pits, and apart from the fact that both are male, the similarities end there. Bob had a very strong effect on my mother, and although I wasn't aware of it at the time, as soon as she started seeing him, she distanced herself from Ian and me. Brenda used to be demonstrative, always ready with hugs and kisses for her boys, but that stopped without warning.

Bob Jones was a big powerful man, who fought as a boxer, and his face showed it. He had a big flat nose, full of blackheads from rubbing it while working in the pit, and he had cauliflower ears which took some getting used to. When I first met him, he made an effort to be nice because I was Brenda's child, but even to my eyes, this made him look clumsy and awkward. Before long I was seeing him regularly, and he would give Ian and me some money to buy sweets at the local shop. On a couple of occasions I saw him in the kitchen kissing Brenda, and I wasn't happy about it, but I didn't associate that with my parents splitting up until much later. She would take us to Bob's house; we would be pushing Lucy in her pushchair, and he would give us coal to take home. It came in small bags and he would give Ian and me fifty pence for our efforts. He always had something to give us.

I can't be sure if he was a chain smoker, but like my mother he was never further than his own reach away from a packet of cigarettes. On the odd occasion when they didn't go out drinking, the two of them would be sat in front of the television, the cloud of smoke obscuring the ceiling above their heads. He was also a man very fond of the horizontal. Ian and I were constantly getting into trouble for making too much noise while Bob was resting. But it didn't matter if he had worked the night shift or not, he would usually be resting.

When he was in the mood for it, he would sometimes listen to Johnny Cash, whereas my mother was more of a Beatles girl. She also liked Cliff Richard, but then so did every other female in the country.

Bob told us we could call him by his name, or we could call him dad. Even though he didn't seem interested in having contact with us, David was still our father, and no-one else deserved to be called dad. Ian and I were not ready to swap Bob for dad as if it made no difference. It did not take long before we got to see the real Bob Jones. He was a smarmy guy who believed people judge books by their cover; so as long as he seemed like an attentive man, then others would see him that way, and not delve any deeper for the truth.

It must have been only a matter of weeks after us moving in with him. He ruled with his fists and this made him the sort of man who was feared but never respected. I can remember the first beating, but I don't know what it was for. There were to be thousands like it, some worse, some not so bad, but there was always a reason for them. If anyone had asked him, in his mind at least, there was justification for them.

I had assumed he had behaved the way he had, because he became responsible for bringing up somebody else's children. Yet when I saw what sort of father he was to his own daughter, it was as clear as day that he treated Ian and me as his own. The only one who escaped the beatings was Lucy. For some reason she was his little princess and he spoilt her rotten. As an adult I got to thinking if maybe my mother's affair with Bob started before we thought it had. But I'm sure Lucy was born before my mum went back to work.

My memories of school, before my childhood came to an end, are mostly good. I started at Keresley Infants School, it was not a big school, but it was a good one, and it was mostly enjoyable. I was a bit of a teacher's pet, forever the goody two-shoes. I remember when Ian started school, that first day he cried his eyes out so the teacher called me to his class to calm him down. I gave him a toy to play with and stayed by him until he settled down. It must have seemed to him as if Brenda had found somewhere to get him out of her way for good.

Every afternoon we would have our free milk and we would listen to a story. Time and time again I would fall asleep while the teacher was reading. It was relaxing to listen to such a calm soothing voice when I knew at home the arguments would be echoing off the walls.

One Christmas we were asked to make a Christmas scene. It was the usual Blue Peter type of thing, sticky back plastic, toilet rolls and yoghurt pots. We all took our turn and stood in front of the whole school during assembly to tell them what was in each of our scenes.

One thing I hated about the school was the fact that the toilets were outside and we had to ask permission if we wanted to go at playtime. We would also have to ask for the toilet roll, which was in fact tracing paper. It didn't matter whether you're a folder or a scruncher, it was noisy and it was considered one of the hazards of playtime. Usually I would be running around, my friends playing with me, and I believe I had a genuine interest in learning.

I had no idea my childhood would end so soon.

Chapter Three

Real Fear

THOSE few moments when the body seems to be both heavy and weightless all at the same time, yet the mind is still active; that time between being aware of what is going on around you, and blissful sleep needs to be savoured by each and every person, every time it occurs. Drifting in and out of consciousness while preparing for rest is a time when the individual feels warm and safe, all worries put aside for the following day.

I can remember that feeling. Yet as I grow older, with each night the memory becomes more and more dim, and all that I can allow myself is an impotent anger toward the one who took my childhood away and, with it, peaceful sleep.

Ison behaved just like everybody else the first time I saw him. He was nice to my brother and me - he brought us sweets – and usually he would give us some sort of toy car to play with. He told us jokes, and he listened to what we had to say. I had never been in a situation where I would be able to recognise a danger sign. But even if I had known what to look out for, there was nothing to be seen.

He was a young man, who seemed to everyone around him to be an amicable and helpful person. My mother saw no reason not to leave her children in his care. Once he had everyone's trust, he knew he could do what he liked.

Ian and I would often bathe together - it saved time and water. We could carry on playing and it never felt like a chore. Brenda was on her way out that evening, and Ison had turned up to sit with us for the evening. We had been playing, and Mum didn't have the patience to wait for us to finish, so Ison said he would get us washed and dressed for bed.

He washed Ian's hair and wiped the suds off his back. Then he rinsed Ian off, and lifted him out of the bath. Standing there, I waited for him to do the same for me. After washing my hair, he decided to wash me a little more carefully. I was shocked - even Brenda, who had bathed me almost every night for the five years of my life thus far, had always used a flannel. It did not seem right to me; no-one had touched me there before, and there had been no reason for it. All the time he said nothing as if this was the most natural thing in the world.

I became wary, uncomfortable with another's touch, frightened I had misread his actions, and frightened I would misunderstand somebody else's behaviour. I also feared why he had done what he had. Not too long after, he came by to sit with us again. I thought I was safe, because mum had already put us to bed. We were wrapped up warm, not quite drifting off to sleep, comfortable and safe in our parents' bed.

Paediatric psychiatrists believe that up to the age of six everything is seen and understood as a game. Ison cut short my play by instilling a fear into me, not just through the abuse he put me through, but also by destroying the only sanctuary a child has to escape to.

Each night I would lie in my parents' bed next to my brother, thinking I would be safe, when in fact I was at my most vulnerable. Once everything was quiet, he would creep into the room and gently search for me under the covers. I do not know which was worse, waking up to the fear and seeing him kneeling by the bed, or just waking up with the fear because I remembered him being there.

A few times I woke up because I had this intense nightmarish feeling that someone was watching me, but usually I would be woken up by Ison masturbating me. Each and every time, he tried to push the boundaries further. It seems each time I tried to refuse, he pointed out that I didn't want to wake Ian up, and that what we did must stay a secret.

He asked me if what he was doing felt nice, and he wanted to know if I had any funny feelings inside. Even if I had known how to describe what I was feeling, I think fear and panic overruled any other feeling and sensation.

Once he thought I was used to his touch, he tried to get me to reciprocate. I didn't understand why it was so important to him; I was only too aware of my fear to try to understand his gratification. This created a lot of confusing and mixed-up signals. Because during the day Ison was nice to me, and I wanted to like him and I guess, like it was expected of most children, I wanted to please him. But every touch made my skin crawl with a fear and dread I could not comprehend. I did not know the mind and body thankfully reject anything that may prove to be dangerous. Scientists call it fight or flight instinct. Small children are naturally scared of growling dogs. The same thing applies to human predators, except children are taught to fight their natural instinct when an adult decides for them it is safe to do so. Yet adults make mistakes and misjudge situations as well as children.

So, two to three times a week, most often at the weekend, Brenda would pay Ison to stay with us while she was off out. Every time it was more or less the same. Like most babysitters, he took advantage of there being no adult supervision and called a friend to stop with him. It was always the same friend. Within ten to perhaps fifteen minutes of my mother leaving, this friend of Ison's would show up. He was always smartly dressed, shirt and trousers, whereas others in the village were happy to be dressed casually for the most part. They both seemed very grown up to me, but neither could have been more than twenty years old when it all started.

They would leave us in the living room and disappear upstairs; sometimes they were gone for ages, but we could usually hear them laughing and joking. Once downstairs again, Ison would offer his friend a cup of tea, but there were times when he just slipped past the door unnoticed.

There were times when he sat with us during the day, and he used to take us to his friend's house, a few streets away. I can remember the door number was sixty-three, because I spent so long looking at it while I was waiting. We would be left standing outside, while he either stayed until he had finished, or he brought his friend back to our house.

I began to dread Ison's visits; it was obvious even to me that he was having fun and he didn't care what he put me through to get it. With each visit to my parents' bed, the list of what he did would grow, and I began to recognise guilt amongst the fear and panic. I began to feel it was somehow my fault that he was doing all that to me. As a five-year-old I still didn't understand the complexities of an adult thought process. With the fear and dread Ison forced upon me, it took me a long time to realise that I had nothing to do with what he put me through. He did not necessarily choose me for me. I did not make him behave the way he did; I was in fact immaterial to what he intended.

Time after time I would wake up to find either his hand or his mouth inside my pyjamas. What amazes me is that even now, I remember the dread that freezes every cell immobile, just lying there like a corpse, the mind screaming to escape and nothing happens. The last breath I took before he neared me, seemed to freeze in my throat, all my muscles tense, the whole body contracted, as if it was trying to hide within itself.

The first time he expected me to become actively involved, I tried even harder to stop him. What he did to me thus far made me feel uncomfortable, guilty, to some extent even tainted. Although I knew he insisted that I tell no-one, I wondered if somehow others could see by my appearance or behaviour, that I was a part of all that. I felt others had started to treat me differently. Imagined or not, I felt Brenda had started behaving differently toward me, towards Ian as well I suppose, but with hindsight I can now see that there were so many things happening, Ison, my parents break-up, Ian starting school, to name a few, that I don't think anyone took any notice of anybody else.

He started masturbating me, and he seemed more talkative than before. Ison wanted to know what I was feeling, and he was telling me that he was having the same feelings as me. At the time I was probably too scared to think anything, but later I thought, if he had the same feeling that I did, why would make us both suffer?

I found that last ounce of strength to sit up, but once I did he growled at me to stop moving. The sound he made was so low that I think I felt it in the air - it seemed inaudible. At the same time, he had slipped his trousers off his hips and started to masturbate himself also. Insisting once again that he felt the same as I did, and then he pulled my hand to his groin. I told him 'No!' This exchange, of him pulling and me refusing, seemed to go on forever, but that evening he gave up and left the room.

I was sadly mistaken in thinking that me saying no would put him off. A few days later, like, by now so many times before, I woke up in my parents' bed. This time he changed tactics and decided to wake me up using fellatio. It was a summer evening, and even though it was around eight maybe nine o'clock, I could see his trousers were crumpled around his knees. Ison was masturbating himself. He only stopped fellating to tell me not to move. After what seemed like an eternity, he just walked out of the room.

An infant's body has no need for sex, and therefore needs no understanding of it. I now know that what Ison did to me, he considered a sexual act. For me it was a phobia-inducing state of terrifying fear that would take years of effort to come to terms with. At the time, I was trying to understand *what* was happening to me, I hoped the answer to *why*, would come later. Just as I began to recognise a pattern, Ison moved the goalposts.

It wasn't long before he decided to teach me the art of masturbation. He woke me up in the usual way, and I saw that he was kneeling by the bed, his trousers by his knees, on the floor. He kept asking me to touch him, and not realising there would be anything else involved, I finally relented. He grabbed my wrist and started to move my hand up and down. I cried; it was the only way I could release the fear, confusion and disgust welling up inside me. He stopped masturbating me, pulled my pyjamas back up, then got dressed himself and left the room.

While David and Brenda had lodgers, there were some who expected food and board, so when that happened, she wouldn't go out so much. This meant that she didn't need a babysitter. Those lodgers inadvertently saved me from some of the abuse.

Days passed into weeks, and the weeks turned into months. The hours seemed endless because I was no more than six or seven when things progressed even further. Not knowing if he was going to sit with us was scary, yet knowing he would soon be here was even worse. Sometimes Brenda didn't tell us she would be going out, so Ison's visits came as a surprise.

Most visits were similar to one another, but some I remember more clearly than others. The first time he removed me from my parents' bed stands out as one such episode. He shook me awake, and then told me, 'Come with me to the next bedroom a minute.' I got out of bed; I remember I was wearing pyjamas with a tie at the waist, not elasticated ones. Before doing anything else I went to the toilet, and headed back into my parents' bedroom, assuming he wanted me to be where he always had.

'No, no, this room,' he said, pointing to my bedroom. Directly behind the door, that is once the door was opened it wasn't visible, stood my bed. There was another just underneath the window. The huge double wardrobe sat by the other side of the door. Ison sat me on my bed and shut the door. He started to untie my pyjamas, and I tried to tell him no. I kept telling him I didn't want to. I must have repeated myself a dozen times before I started crying. All he could reply was, 'It ain't going to hurt.'

He stood up in front of me, dropping his trousers, revealing a now familiar and dreaded bulge behind his light blue Y-fronts. I can remember they had white piping all around the edges. They too dropped to the floor. He took my hand, and placed it where he wanted it. I kept pulling it back; all I could do was sob.

He was getting annoyed by this point. Without warning he grabbed me by the arm and flung me into the wardrobe, locking me in. Like a rag doll, I hit the back of it as I heard the key turn in the lock. I gulped air as the darkness swallowed me up. With my lungs full to capacity, I started screaming for him to let me out. I didn't want to make a compromise, but I knew Ison had complete control of the situation. He kept saying over and over again that he would let me out if I did as I was told. I had no choice, either stay in the wardrobe, hoping my parents would know where to find me, or do what he asked. Time must flow differently inside a locked wardrobe, to me it seemed I had been in there for hours, but he let me out after about ten minutes.

Let out, may not be the best description. He was still angry, so he pulled me by the arm and dragged me out, sending me flying onto my bed. Again he kept repeating, 'If you don't do as you're told, you'll go back into the wardrobe.' This tirade continued with descriptions of all the bad things that would happen to me if I didn't do what he wanted, and especially if I told anyone. I was absolutely petrified.

He asked if I was going to do what he said, but he made it perfectly clear that I had no choice. He pressed down on my shoulders, forcing me to sit. Ison dropped his trousers to the floor, and told me what to do. I was crying the whole time; it was almost as if he didn't notice or didn't care that I was upset, as long as I continued to masturbate him. He said that I should put it into my mouth, and even before I had the chance to say no, his hand was on the back of my neck, pulling me towards his genitals. Momentarily I had stopped crying, and I was using both hands to push him away from me. The thought of what he wanted was so repulsive that I knew I had to try anything to stop him. Angrily, he sat on the bed next to me and said, 'This is what you're supposed to do.' He lifted his top and vest, catching them in his teeth to keep them out of the way. He lay down and masturbated to ejaculation.

As I saw this sticky substance spurt onto his stomach, I felt the room spinning; everything around me was becoming black and white, and I knew I was falling to the floor. I woke up the next morning, with no idea of how I got into my own bed, who put me there, or what had happened since the last thing I remembered seeing.

Mothers have an uncanny feeling and are able to recognise when there is something not quite right with their child. That morning, while we sat down to breakfast, Brenda asked me what was wrong. Perhaps in the light of day, Ison's threats did not seem as daunting, so I blurted it all out. Yet she said nothing. That same evening he stopped by again.

Perhaps a week later, she decided to talk to me about what I'd told her. Just out of the blue, with nothing in the conversation before to suggest she had anything to say on the matter, she kept her opinion short and sweet, and made it perfectly clear there was no need for me to respond.

'What you told me the other day about Ison, you mustn't tell anyone else about it, and we're not going to talk about it again.'

The one person who led me to believe would be there for me, turned me away, ignoring my plea. From that moment on, I knew I would be alone, and that I must cope alone. Most of my childhood from then on only reinforced that belief.

Although I still called her Mum, with that sentence she uttered while we walked back from Nan's, she became just Brenda. She was someone who lived in the same house, cooked and cleaned for me until I was old enough to fend for myself; the relationship had ended. Looking back, I can tell that she withdrew all affection from Ian and me when she met Bob, but at the time it was so easy for me to assume that this had happened because of what I had told her.

When a child thinks a parent is disgusted with its actions, the child will feel guilt and remorse. My mother's reaction made me sure more than ever that I was to blame for what was happening. I did as she asked, and Ison was never mentioned again.

For the next four, maybe five years, the abuse continued relentlessly. He would wake me up and take me into the next room in order to abuse me. If at any time I refused, he would put me into the wardrobe. That used to happen often. He forced me more and more often to perform oral sex. If for some reason he didn't ejaculate into my mouth, he would do so onto anything to hand, usually a vest or some other piece of clothing.

I began to suffer from blackouts more and more frequently. I was aware of the sensation of all sounds and smells fading; my eyes would stop focusing and I would only see black and white spots in front them. Everything around me would blend in a swirl. It was as if my mind had created a tornado to destroy my world, and I was in its eye, safe. Except it was only in my mind, and the real world waited for me when I came to. At school, there was one teacher in particular who I remember getting me out of view from the other children. Her name was Mrs Hamilton, and she showed every child equal attention as it was needed. She would often carry me out of the classroom.

My mother decided it would be for the best if I went to see the doctor. The man could have been using telepathy in order to make a diagnosis. Following my conversation with Brenda, only my Grandmother's passing away was given as the cause of stress.

Back in the wardrobe, things were getting worse. It seemed every time he locked me in, something even more horrific would be waiting for me outside. There was no more abuse in my parents' bedroom; he shook me awake, and took me by the hand into my own room. If I was lucky he would let me be, afterwards, and I could rest in my own bed. Somehow it was worse when he took me back to lie next to my brother, so my parents would find me where they expected me to be, and it would give the impression that nothing had happened.

He would often return the favour, so to speak, as if him masturbating me made the other acts less abusive. With the fear he had created and perpetuated, I knew I didn't want to touch anyone else, nor did I want anyone else touching me.

I must have been around nine years old when Ison first attempted to have intercourse with me. It all started in the usual way; I stood in the dark room, the shapes of the furniture becoming familiar as my eyes grew accustomed to the little light there was. The big wardrobe loomed to the side of me, and I could feel the bed covers through my pyjama bottoms. He started to masturbate me, and then I had to do the same to him. It was the same for oral sex. Then he told me he wanted to try something new. I knew I was scared, but I had no idea of what. Perhaps that was what had scared me more. I turned around, my back to him, only after he threatened to lock me in the wardrobe.

He pushed my back down, so I was bent over the bed. He picked up a babies' brush from the table. It must have been Lucy's. It was one of those white plastic ones with soft bristles that were almost translucent in colour. My pyjama bottoms were somewhere around my ankles, my bare knees pressing on the edge of the mattress. Ison tried to push the brush handle into me, but instinctively I moved away. He tried again, and this time his hand gripped my shoulder harder to keep me in place. Even before the brush handle was inside my anus, I began crying, knowing my tears would have no effect whatsoever. By the time he took the brush handle out I was sobbing hysterically. He moved closer to me, ignoring my pleas and cries, and I could feel his trouser zip scratching my calf. Holding on to me, he tried to position himself as best he could. I begged for him to stop, but by now I must have been much louder than before because he just kept repeating for me to shut up. I felt a stretching, burning pain that seemed to sear throughout my intestines all the way into my stomach. He must have tried to create some friction, but he came out at which point I felt a hot sticky liquid spill down my spine. I lay in bed trying to cry myself to sleep. It seemed a long way off.

The next morning, once I got to the bathroom, I was still in pain, wary about sitting down, and when I wiped myself there was blood on the paper. I went downstairs, wondering if anyone would notice - if anyone would do anything to stop it happening again. I felt different, so I just assumed my family either saw it and chose to ignore it, or even worse, they had no idea, and I had already been warned not to mention it any more.

For some reason he left me alone for two weeks, which was a long time for Ison. In fact during that fortnight he didn't visit at all. When he returned he brought me a lucky bag and a toy tank. I was too caught up in my own disastrous life to worry about anyone else, but I have a feeling Ison didn't baby-sit with Lucy. Perhaps Brenda thought she was too small to be left alone with anyone, and she was closer to Lucy than to her boys.

Ison had stopped the abuse. Or so I thought. There had been three visits since the two-week break. On that third visit, his friend showed up. The two of them disappeared upstairs, leaving Ian and me downstairs. I needed to use the bathroom, so I headed up the staircase and once I had finished I walked into my own room. On my bed, the two of them lay naked top to tail. I recognised what they were doing to each other because by now I had been subjected to the same hundreds of times over the past four years.

He saw me, and they jumped away from each other. Ison sat me between them. 'It's okay; sit here.' Both of them were naked, both had erections. Ison introduced me to his friend, even telling me his name; I heard it, but I wasn't listening. Again I felt I had something to fear. Once the threats to go into the wardrobe had been repeated a couple of times, as well as a threat of being hit, I followed Ison's instructions and had to perform fellatio on his friend. His friend preferred a 'hands on' approach, and masturbated as well, before ejaculating into my mouth. He may have said something to me, but I was petrified, so I don't remember. Then it was Ison's turn, and once he'd had enough, he sent me downstairs.

This same scenario happened on a couple more occasions, but neither used force, although the usual threats were made. The third time, I had decided enough was enough, and I packed my bag. I picked up a couple of pillows, and simply told my mother that I was leaving home. There wasn't much of a reaction, and she didn't ask why, nor did I think I could tell her; she had made her opinion crystal clear. I sat on the grass verge outside, and I cried. The tears flowed until my father came home, and he must have assumed that it was the normal type of running away that most children attempt at some point. He realised that it was something more serious, because he could see I was becoming hysterical at the thought of going back into the house.

That afternoon, my parents had a huge row, and my Dad actually started questioning why Ison was babysitting so often. The whole situation seemed to implode with that one argument, as David must have realised Brenda was seeing Bob. She must have made some effort, but it proved too little too late, and as far as her marriage was concerned, it was just cosmetic. She must have told Ison she didn't need his services any more, and a young girl sat with us for a while. She lasted a few months, and then Brenda brought Ison back.

My mother is either an evil woman who enjoyed watching her child suffer, or just plain stupid if she didn't realise I had told her the truth. She sent me to his house, so I could ask him if he would like to come and sit with Ian and me. I hated her, I hated him, but most of all, I hated myself for not being able to do anything to stop what was about to happen.

He only babysat on maybe three more occasions, and each time he had abused me. One time, he made another attempt to bugger me, but he didn't use any implements. I was just as distraught as the last time, but he just dismissed me. He behaved toward me as if it was my fault that he failed to have intercourse.

We saw less of any babysitter from then on, as Brenda started taking us with her on her visits to Bob. It seems that within days we moved out, leaving my father, and our new life was about to start.

Chapter Four

Life with Bob

BRENDA had made up her mind. We were going to live with Bob, and we could even call him Dad. What nonsense, I don't even think Lucy, who was about six years old, could mistake Bob for Dad. Luckily, he understood, and to some extent, was probably pleased that we wanted to call him Bob.

We were happy with the distance this created between us. After all, we were only a few streets away from the house we shared with our father, and we knew how to get there if we wanted to. Brenda had promised that she would take us to see him whenever we wanted, but it was when the two of them were at each other's throats the minute they caught sight of each other, that it proved difficult. I could see that they weren't happy together, but I couldn't help wishing they would be. Perhaps away from him, she would be more like her old self. I missed my Dad; I would sit and daydream how, any minute now, he would show up and take us all back. Oblivious to everything around me, my mind completely blank, I am unaware of everything until...

Someone shaking me by the shoulder; without looking I sense Ison's arm. He's pulling me up, wants me in the other room. I open my eyes, and gulp air, as I force my brain to realise I'm sitting in Bob's house, and Ison isn't around. Only it's Ian, asking me if I want my tea.

At first, Bob made an effort in between punishments to show us some sort of attention by giving us sweets, but all that I could think was that he wanted the same as Ison. He would buy us the same sorts of sweets, and for a long time I couldn't even look at a Curley Wurley without cringing. Like Pavlov's dogs, every time I was handed some sweets, an icy sweat would trickle down my spine, my skin crawling with fear and expectation.

In my bedroom, I had a chest of drawers and it was huge. It had four drawers, and there was always one that was empty. Or at least until I started to hide all the sweets I'd been given. Most of my friends couldn't get enough of sweets and chocolates, but they all associated them with good times and happy memories. I, on the other hand, fought to keep my stomach contents in place every time I opened the drawer.

Someone hands me a bag of sweets, my tongue tingles with anticipation for the sugary taste. I really, really want to savour them. Each one, one after the other, until I bloat and settle into a glucose-induced stupor. The voice in my head screams the sweets will cost me, every one is an IOU, a favour owing for later. My skin shivers, the cold coming from the inside, the sort of cold that has no source, no beginning or end, and no amount of heat from the outside will shift it.

But life was very much like it had been with Brenda before we left. She would assume that if she ignored whatever was going on, it would stop or sort itself out. For the sake of appearances, she didn't like to rock the boat, so I always felt nothing would change if she were involved. Lucy was growing, although we never seemed to have much to do with her. Maybe it was the age difference, maybe we were painfully aware that she was shown more affection, or maybe it was just because she was a girl. Brenda would brush her hair while we got ready for school.

The cold white plastic brush handle prising open my buttocks. My lower lip quivers, as I catch sight of Ian doing his shoelaces, and I know I must stay strong, I must ignore the memories intruding into my thoughts.

A few days would pass, and everything would seem normal. The nights were a different matter. Although I knew Ison didn't know where I slept, he had no idea which room was mine, the nightmares would rage in front of my eyes, from short images, like photographs or sound-bites, to me having to watch whole episodes of abuse as if it had happened to someone else. Even though it was my brain and I should have been able to control what thoughts went through it, every single night my mind was imprisoned by the traumas of abuse.

Bob was far too busy and far too important as the head of a new household to have a real relationship with his stepsons. His way of thinking was that we ought to be grateful he was providing a roof over our heads and the food that we ate. It soon became clear that we were insignificant little creatures who just got in the way. Constantly he would growl at us through his clenched and nicotine stained teeth to keep out, or to keep quiet, or to sit still, or whatever we were doing wrong.

It took us maybe a fortnight to realise we shouldn't sit within arm's reach as we had with my dad. Ian and I were used to the physical distance kept between Brenda and us, and I suppose we had hoped now that we had the chance to start again, she might love us the way she had before. We saw her every day, but she seemed so out of our reach. It didn't take us much longer than that to realise when we were within reach, he would re-enforce his barks with a punch or a slap. This seemed like the safer option though because if ever he believed we were trying to avoid his punishment, we would be hit for that as well.

I hear laughter from a room upstairs, and every hair on my body stands on end as I can feel my pyjama bottoms loosening at the waist. I look down and I can see my legs are in my school trousers, so I realise nothing is happening to me. But I check my waistband just to make sure and all I can feel, wherever I touch, are goose pimples.

When he worked the night shift, we had to be quiet the whole day, whether he was asleep or not. He would spend most of his spare time either prostrate at home, or drinking at the pub. So we only really saw him when he was eating with the family or when he needed to punish us. School friends did the same things as me, but never mentioned the sorts of punishments I was getting. I wish I could say he was fair and punished us when we broke a window or damaged something, but even then, we were still too young to do these sorts of things on purpose. Both Ian and I had the mindset of naïve children who didn't wish to hurt anyone or damage anything intentionally. Bob did not think of us as children who still needed to learn the difference between right and wrong, but assumed we had the full faculties of an adult, and therefore everything we did only served for us to wind him up.

I made lots of friends while I was living in Thompson Road, but I was mostly a loner. I would like to be able to say I liked my own company, but I had very little opportunity to escape my memories. My first trip to the cinema was one such opportunity; it was overwhelming whilst I was under its influence. I sat through the film, forgetting who I was and what had happened to me. The film was Born Free, and everything within it was different to my life. The sights, the sounds, I could even imagine the smells of the savannah first thing in the morning. I could almost feel soft warm fur beneath my fingers as I wondered what it would be like to stroke a lion cub.

Once outside in the dreary reality of my home town, the film was nothing in my life, a little time out, and some entertainment that made a part of the day more pleasant. Fishing was something that I liked. It gave me something simple to focus on. Humans and their emotions were so complicated, and the very real, yet somehow at the same time, surreal interactions I experienced at home were scary. With time, these relationships I had with Brenda and Bob would become normal only because they would go on for so long. Yet at the beginning, when I could still remember how it had been, how my life had started, I felt that I was mourning.

The wardrobe closes in; the darkness swallows me up as I try not to imagine who is on the other side. When I dare to open my eyes, I expect the dark, but what I see is a different type of dark, because I'm sitting on a grass verge, and the sun had hidden behind a cloud.

It was rare for me not to catch anything. It really didn't matter even if I didn't. I can't imagine a fisherman considering any trip a waste if he came back with nothing. Fishing is not about catching fish. It is all about the process of setting up, calming down, and waiting for something to grab the hook. Some people meditate, others smoke, but I used to fish. School was another nightmare I used to escape from by the pond.

By the time I got to junior school, I was having serious problems interacting with anyone. It was difficult enough trying to cope with what was going on inside my head, as well as at home, without having to deal with being put under pressure to learn and take information in and make use of it instantly.

Some people say there is no such thing as dyslexia, that it is only a matter of teaching, that it is a claim made by the lazy - either staff who can't be bothered to teach, or children who do not wish to learn. From personal experience, I know it is neither, because I had good teachers and I wanted to learn. Yet I was constantly under pressure, and no matter how they presented the information, I struggled to keep it in. I found it easier to copy, and if I watched, I would be able to do the same quickly and competently. But even if I had been able to keep up, the stress and trauma had destroyed my confidence, so my formal education only took me so far.

I smell him close to me, his breath on my cheek as he leans in to kiss me good night, I hear Ian's sleepy breath nearby, and I shudder knowing this will happen again. I shake away the feeling, but it clings to me and I sit down. The changing room is empty; all the other boys have gone out onto the field and my arms are getting cold because I had taken my arms out of the sleeves; the tee-shirt is hanging around my neck. I have no idea how long I'd been standing there.

I hated sports, both team games and individual events, and I only got involved because everybody had to. Playing rounders was probably the only thing I liked. We would be split into four teams, named red, blue, yellow, and green, and each team member would be given a coloured rubber ring which we would wear on our shoulder, so everyone knew who was playing for which team.

I liked history, geography as well, but I would have preferred to be doing something, not just sitting in a classroom. I guess I never took to theories;I was enthusiastic about gaining information but I had to be close to what was being explained. It had no effect, the teacher explaining the difference between clay and sandstone, when I couldn't see it for myself. Also I had the feeling I was trapped when I was sitting behind a desk.

I was considered unruly, especially in school, and I suppose that was because I spent more time there than anywhere else. That was until I realised I could escape. It didn't matter where I was, or what was going on, it was just as likely for me to get a nosebleed as it was for me to pass out. There would be a torrent of blood flowing from my nose that seemed to go on forever. Unlike passing out, there seemed to be no warning for the nose-bleeds. This was yet another reason why I didn't form many relationships with others. Not just friendships, but working or learning relationships that perhaps would have helped me get on a bit better at school.

Bob was determined to make sure I would behave as he expected, however many punches it would take. Before long, he had a brainwave; Ian and I would earn our keep. Like my father, he worked in the pits, and like most of the employees he could see there was a lot of wastage, and the amounts being shipped out so huge that a bag disappearing here and there wouldn't be noticed.

Again, I knew this wasn't right. Just like Ison's abuse, I knew instinctively that I didn't want to be involved. This put me in a situation where I would have to accept his blows, as well as having to steal. I suppose this part of our relationship was what other children shared with their fathers or stepfathers. It was the only real interaction I had with him. He taught me how to steal coal, and I learnt quickly. I guess I wanted to please him. I thought if he was happy with me, then perhaps the beatings wouldn't happen so often. I didn't understand the two had nothing to do with each other.

Bob would tell us that we were taking from the state, which didn't provide what it had promised, and no-one would notice the little we took compared to what was being mined daily. He would take us to the pits, usually in the dark. Once I was in a routine, I could carry away up to 2 tons a night. Depending on where we would enter, Bob would either throw us over the fence, or widen the gap in the fence so we could get inside. At first we carried a bag each, Bob taking most of what we brought out. As we got stronger, he expected us to carry more and more. Each bag, the small ones that is, weighed twenty-five kilograms, so about fifty-five pounds. By the time I got to puberty, I often carried two hundred kilos at a time, without getting out of breath. In my teens I realised that crime does not pay, but it can help you get into good condition.

Trapped inside the wardrobe, a cold sweat trickles down my spine as I feel a heavy weight pressing on my chest. Bob moves the fence panel, letting some light in, I realise where I am, and that the weight is a sack of coal.

Bob was always a safe distance away; he wasn't the sort of man who would get his fingers dirty, at least not figuratively. After years in the pits, his pores and creases were permanently tinged with grey and black. This made him look even more sinister. When I had the chance to read Charles Dickens' *Oliver*, and even more so when I saw the film with Oliver Reed, I couldn't help but associate his image with that of Bill Sykes.

Brenda made the effort to have dinner on the table for us every night, but we were never allowed to graze or nibble, because there wasn't enough food for that. I remember getting a beating for taking some cheese from the fridge. It wasn't for stealing, which is what Bob had told me, but for being stupid enough to leave my teeth marks in the slab I put back. He made a big thing about it, ordering Ian and me to stand to attention, and then making us show him our teeth from all sides, so he would be able to see who had bitten into the cheese. He must have known it was me; from an early age I loved any kind of cheese, and I could eat it by the inch. It was just his way of prolonging the punishment.

My legs start to shake, my skin crawls and I can see Ison's hand rubbing my thigh, the taste of chocolate clings to my mouth, and feels like a bribe. Before I realise what is happening, I sit down on a wall, and I see a Mars bar in my shaking hand. I spin around to see if anyone is about, but I'm completely alone.

One good memory I have of school is a camping trip I took with my class. It was only the usual of cold nights crammed into tents, sitting by a fire, telling silly ghost stories, followed by the really scary ones, and eating burnt sausages and cold baked beans. We sang songs, relaxed, and slept relatively well. Apart from the rare night of peace, most mornings I would feel more tired than I did when I got into bed. Sleeping in the dark had its own consequences, yet a nightlight created shadows I wanted to avoid. The smell of freshly laundered bedding would sometimes be a comfort, at least on a physical level. It was always comfortable to settle into cool sheets, if I had been battered about. Bob was heavy handed and impulsive. As long as everything was as he wanted, the day would pass peacefully. It just never happened.

I gave up trying to understand why I was being hit. If I wanted to escape serious injury, I would just have to avoid anything that might set him off. As the bruises proved, this was more difficult than I imagined. What had been safe the previous day could mean an even worse beating the following day.

I took advantage of having to change schools, and I determined a new start would mean an end to the old. So I spent more and more time away. It got to a point where we were almost on first name terms with the truancy officer. Mr West would come by and, before long, he was just Mr West; he had no need to say what he was doing or why he was there. Truancy was not the answer to my problems; I suppose it was a cry for attention. Sometimes it felt like I was dreaming, dreaming I was stuck in a world where I understood what others were saying to me, but when I opened my mouth, they wouldn't understand what I was saying. Like the night terrors that would wake me, leaving me covered in icy droplets of sweat and paralysed except for the one thought of 'must escape, must escape, must escape', whirling through my mind.

Escaping school did not allow me to get away from my memories or my cuts and bruises. It would at least give me some space to get away from other people. There was never any break from the intrusions, whether from inside my head or from those around me. Once I realised no-one was going to help me, in my own defiant way I dismissed any structure offered by society, and made my own way. So I would leave the house, and head for the woods or the river. And because everyone else was leaving at the same sort of time, at least one person would see me head off, and of course they would tell Bob.

For a while, Mr West made a special effort; he would go to all my usual haunts, and wait for me, then escort me back to school. This usually meant that he would bring me to one gate, and I would slink off to the other and disappear before he could get there ahead of me.

I don't remember Bob coming out to look for me, but when I walked through the front door, sometimes I wouldn't have time to see, it would be more or less a sensation of a fist flying toward my face, and then nothing. So many times my first view of the house interior was the blurred smoky hallway ceiling. Those were the good times. There were days when he would be at work, so Bob would wake me up to beat me when he got home. This was a chore to him, and getting me out of bed just prolonged the process. As the back of his hand made contact with one side of my face, my eyes and my brain ricocheting against my skull, it wasn't unusual for me to bounce off the wall behind me, bruising my shoulder and hitting the other side of my head as well. It must be instinctive, but I always seemed to move closer to a wall, or something solid that would shield at least one side of me.

There were other times, when he would leave me be until the following morning. Waiting was never easy. I tried to be brave and take my punishment like I was expected to, but so often I had no idea what it was for. There were times when I would genuinely sit dazed, trying to remember why I had deserved such a beating.

Sometimes, he thought he should make the effort to explain, which meant that each syllable would equate to a slap or punch. Think-be-fore-you-do-any-thing-boy. You-on-ly-have-your-self-to-blame. Do-not-let-me-catch-you-do-ing-that-a-gain! Normally though, he would be quiet.

On the odd occasion, I knew exactly what was coming to me and why. I don't know how it happened, but the aerial on the roof was bent, so I had the idea that if I threw a brick tied with string over the roof, I could catch the aerial and straighten it. Genius. The picture was always blurred, and all the faces were wonky. Once, twice, and the third time it got over. Except I threw it with a little too much enthusiasm, and the brick flew over the roof, and down past the upstairs window, and straight through the downstairs window, to swing inches away from Bob's face. Although I was at the front of the house when I heard the glass pane smash, from the amount of noise Bob was making I assumed the brick must have knocked ash off the end of his cigarette. I know exactly why I was beaten that time - I interrupted his dinner. I can only imagine what his face must have looked like as the brick flew into view, and then into his dinner. Splat!

The image in my mind's eye is clear as he always followed the same routine. He sat at the table, looking out into the back garden, his dinner plate exactly in front of him, a huge mug of tea to the side, and an ashtray next to it. I know the brick landed in his plate, because he stormed out of the front door, his dinner dripping down his shirt. He started after me, in just his socks, but I took off. When I returned home, Bob and Brenda had gone out drinking for the night, so my beating was postponed until Bob dragged me from my bed when he returned home.

There are things that a child shouldn't decide; fixing the television picture is one, and education is another. Obviously I shouldn't have cut school. But in my defence, at the time I felt I had no other option. If Bob had talked to me, well, I would have been very surprised, but never the less, I think I would have made an effort if I believed someone had my interest at heart. Even Mr West, who had made such an effort, was only doing his job; he couldn't afford to get involved with every child who wagged from school.

Brenda just wanted me to keep the peace. I think she worried more about how my actions reflected on her, than what I may have been going through. What the neighbours thought was an important issue. Who told on me was often more disturbing to them than the actual truancy.

Between them, they were unable to come up with a suitable deterrent. Even blizzards and icy roads didn't stop me. After all, no physical cold could compare to the fear filling each and every cell of my being with cold until it was ready to burst. No matter what the weather, I found myself walking, or once I'd found a suitable spot, I would settle for a while, either nursing my bruises, or fighting my demons. The time would pass slowly as I walked through the woods and the surrounding countryside. When I managed to focus on what was around me, I would just stop and stare at the myriad shades of green. I was fascinated by what nature had placed before me. The trees loomed powerful and strong above me, the gentle blades of grass swayed with the breeze, not a care in the world. I wished I could have been a blade of grass, or even a tall and strong tree. I didn't consider I was wasting my time, yet there were also days when I lost time. Wandering around for hours, I would suddenly realise I had just returned from a flashback, with no idea what I had re-lived, nor knowing what the trigger had been.

These were difficult moments, because I learnt to recognise some triggers, and I was able to avoid them. Sweets and chocolates were one, hairbrushes were another, cold weather, and ice especially would leave me dazed, and unsure of where I was. So not knowing what I needed to avoid made me anxious.

Being in bed was another thing I tried to avoid. If I didn't rest properly, Bob's blows would seem harder and more painful. Recovering from each beating would also take longer. I suppose instinctively I made sure my body was healthy and capable, and I knew rest was crucial to my survival. I usually succeeded in keeping out of his way, but sometimes Bob would catch me off guard, and it would take me days to recover from a beating. What was worse, was knowing I had to stay in bed for the duration.

In his anger, Bob would not only lash out with slaps and punches, but he used to grab whatever was within reach - a belt, a cane, a poker. Sometimes the only thing he could use was a wall. Holding me by the shoulders, he would tip me back violently so my head would thud against the wall, my legs buckling underneath me in an instant.

There was one occasion when he beat Ian with a poker, and by the time Bob had finished, it was obvious that the split skin, welts, and swellings would need professional attention. His stay in hospital shocked us all, but it wasn't to be the last. For a while at least, Bob kept his distance, but once Ian had recovered it was all back to normal. Sometimes the welts were in a natural crease, and they seemed to take forever to heal. Choosing a position to sleep in had become a bit of an art, as the raised and angry purple reminder growls and shrieks for its own breathing space.

I'm hoping things would be different now, that medical staff would recognise injuries for what they are, but when Bob and Brenda took him into hospital, they told the doctors he had fallen down the stairs, and nothing more was said about it.

Ison came by to see us, bringing sweets. He had spoken to Brenda, who obviously thought it would be wonderful for us to spend some time with him. Ian had been hinting to me that he felt uncomfortable around Ison, which meant that my hatred was even more justified, because my brother didn't like him either. I was too caught up in my own fear and pain to consider what anyone else had suffered. I must have been an adult when I realised what he had told me, and it was only when I plucked up sufficient courage to write that we got to talking.

It was about this time that the cat, which had adopted us, had kittens. I loved to watch her with her tiny bundles of squeaking fur. She was a loving, caring, and careful mother. Each one of the kittens would be licked clean, and then they would all nestle beside her where they were warm and safe. As one by one they opened their eyes, they stared with fascination at everything around them. Soon they would start to explore; the impatience showed in their bright and curious eyes.

Once they started to explore, it was more and more difficult to hide them. Their mother's milk wasn't enough, and there seemed so many mouths to feed. I wanted to provide for them, but Bob's budget did not allow for so many pets, and he told me in no uncertain terms, that if I were unable to feed them, I would have to do the most responsible thing in such a situation.

I looked down at those five pairs of big round eyes that took up so much space in the heads that were three times bigger than the body, and I started to make a mental list of all my friends who may want a kitten, but Bob made the responsible decision for me. He stood behind me; the refuse sack in his hand rustled, and I realised my friends would not watch my kittens try to run, and then comically lose balance because the head is too heavy for its neck.

The walk from the kitchen to the dining room had never seemed so long. My heart was heavy; my legs seemed even heavier. Carrying a hundred kilograms of coal was like a feather compared to that bucket. I think had I been frog-marched to my own death, those five minutes would have passed much faster.

Bob just stood there and watched. I had no choice; it had been implied that it was either the kittens or me. Knowing what Bob was capable of, it didn't take much fear and imagination to conclude he could do to a child what he wanted me to do to the kittens. I put my hand into the big black bag, and my fingers felt the soft warm fur. Innocent and naive, they let out little squeaks; still too young to miaow, my familiar hand poses an unrecognised threat. If I held my hands outstretched, each one could have laid across my palms safely supported. I didn't dare. I looked at Bob, not sure what I ought to do. I didn't know where to start.

There was only one person I really wanted to hurt, but I never considered what it would take to extinguish a life. Should I strangle each one first before holding them under the water, or just hold them until they stop wriggling? The white kitten looked up at me as the water in the bucket rose around it. Without blinking it stared sadly at me, its legs trying to push the water away. My eyes blurred with tears I should have kept for later. I realised Bob thought of me as weak, because I wasn't able to do this without emotion. The kittens were growing accustomed to the bag, and it seemed to me they were playing. Bob stood there, an impatient look on his face; he grew more and more uncomfortable, the longer it took. I had to fight myself to do what he asked; the guilt was overwhelming. How would I be able to look that cat in the eyes, knowing what I had to do to her litter? She carried them safely through pregnancy, gave birth to them, fed and cleaned them, and when the time came for her to teach them to fend for themselves, I drown them. Dragging my feet out of the dining room was when I realised that inflicting pain and misery was worse than having to suffer it. I made a conscious decision that whenever possible I would do what I could never to hurt anyone again, and also I would never again allow anyone to hurt me.

A warm furry ball nestles into my hands; I feel my body dropping into the sludge at the bottom of the pond. My mind is racing but it is a futile gesture. I close my eyes as I release my last breath, and then panic. Everything is black; I'm sinking into the thick black mud below me, and my lungs scream with pain. I try to lift myself up, but I can't. If I lean on an elbow, I'll drop the kitten. Somewhere deep inside I find the strength I need to lift my head and shoulders, and the duvet slips off the bed. I jump so violently, that I wake Ian up.

Luckily the dining room was very rarely used; we tended to eat from our laps in the living room. The dining room was for formal occasions only, and even then us children didn't spend much time there. I was thankful that I didn't have to remember the bucket of cold water every time I ate.

The next time I saw Ison, he had a puppy with him. It was a gift for me; he wanted us to be friends again. I took the puppy, or more to the point, the puppy took to me. Perhaps because all his other gifts had been inanimate objects, I was able to separate the dog from Ison. I called him Blacky. It was an easy choice of name, because I think he approved. He loved the water, but that was to be expected from a Labrador, although Blacky was actually a cross breed. He was half Doberman, half Labrador. So he was playful and loyal, but had no qualms about showing aggression if he thought he would have to protect me.

From the moment he saw me, I understood he wanted to be a friend. I was aware of the fact that Blacky was a dog, and couldn't understand English, yet when it came to emotions and feelings, he could recognise them in an instant. I suppose animals are just like small children, they can pick up the slightest change in someone's mood.

We were inseparable. Blacky was happy to walk by my side for however long I needed, and he never let me see if he got bored with waiting for me to take him home. At last I had found a companion for whom I didn't have to pretend. No matter what she would ask me, I always felt as if I was lying to Brenda, because she refused to hear the truth. My father wasn't around, and even if he was, I don't think I was willing to risk the same sort of reaction as I had from Brenda. Bob ignored us unless there was something he wanted us to do. Ian seemed an introvert, not the type to have a discussion about anything. This does not mean he didn't care; he just didn't get involved in conversations very much.

So Blacky was probably the only good friend in my life. He had a calming effect on me; the anger I had didn't disappear, but he just made it possible for me to cope with it a little easier. The time I spent with him was well spent, and I started to enjoy myself, for a few hours a day at least. He also allowed me to make use of the courage I didn't know I had. For a long time before Blacky came along, I was sure I had no choice but to put up with what life had thrown in front of me. With my new friend by my side, I felt I had more control; I could make decisions for myself.

Chapter Five

Father Figure

I DIDN'T have the opportunity to meet many people while I was wandering around, which I suppose was a blessing. Most of the people I did see were like me, avoiding contact and interaction with others. Often I would go past the pits, hoping I would get to see my dad, but knowing if he was around he was probably several hundred feet down. In a field nearby, there was a caravan that looked as if it were ready to fall apart. The man who owned it was much the same. I never was able to find out much about his life before he moved there, but he gave the impression that he was actually an intelligent man; there would always be someone around talking to him, asking for advice.

His name was Ivan, and although scruffy, he was genuine when it came to the people he chose to befriend. Ivan's shirts were all threadbare, and his trousers seemed stretched around the back, and I'm sure every morning his belly would be squashed into his trousers, but little by little, it would escape so that by the end of the day it would be hanging precariously over the waistband.

Ivan was a chubby man with a friendly smile, and everybody liked him. He used to work as a rag and bone man. He had a pony and cart, but he also kept donkeys which would graze all around the caravan. I don't think there was an animal he didn't know how to care for. It wasn't so much that he collected them; they just sort of made their own way. Much like the kids he took under his wing. The caravan itself was musty and had a damp smell, much like Ivan, but in a cramped sort of way, it was homely. It was always untidy, but everyone was welcome there.

No-one ever objected to my friendship with him, probably because everyone knew him, and I could be found easily if I was with him. He never minded my questions; he was always happy to explain what he was doing, and asking me to help him, rather than telling me what I had to do.

Like all the other men in and around the village, Ivan would have a drink in the Golden Eagle pub. Lots of people knew him from before he moved into the caravan. I heard stories about him living in a house, and that he had been successful, but I never found out why he lived by the pit, or why he was alone. He never once mentioned a family to me, so I didn't know whether he had been married or whether he was a father.

Because I missed so much school, one day was much like any other; I didn't differentiate between a weekday and the weekend. Ivan would wait for me on a Sunday morning, and just as it was getting light, we would head out into the countryside to look for rabbits. I would take Blacky with me, and some days we walked for miles without noticing the distance until I got home and sat down. Ivan made an effort with me by allowing me a sense of achievement. He made sure we never came back empty-handed, and sometimes we would even have rabbits to sell to others.

Most often we would go rabbiting. We kept ferrets, as did Ivan, and each time we took them with us, he would give me hints and tips on how to work with them. He was always willing to explain what could go wrong and how I could avoid the common mistakes, and the more time I spent with him, the quicker I learnt how to hunt. There were occasions when we would smoke them out, but I never quite got the hang of that. I enjoyed working with dogs, and I became comfortable around animals, whereas it took me forever to get used to people.

It was also fun preparing for a poaching session, because we would sit in the caravan, and Ivan would give me some simple task, like counting out the currants, or cutting the horsehair, and while he was getting all the other things together, he would be talking constantly, telling me about poaching from days gone by, and how he learnt what he was now teaching me.

Ivan spent a lot of time taking care of his traps, showing me how they must be cleaned and where they should be kept. He was always very careful, and I think more so when there was someone around. Safety was important to him. He was more like my father than Bob had ever tried to be, and I appreciate that he was willing to spend his time with me.

Ivan had a friendly voice that carried well, but he also knew how to speak clearly whenever he needed to whisper. When we set out the traps, he would tell me all his tales of brave poachers who were as cunning as the animals and even more cunning than other hunters. Sometimes I was sure he had mixed up his stories of real people he had met and known with fairy tales and legends. Often there would be a Robin Hood type character that would help the downtrodden whilst showing the whole world how bad the baddies were. These would be intertwined with information that he passed on to me about what we were doing. I suppose he tried to make the learning a little more fun than just instruction.

He taught me how to put a drizzle of honey on the edge of an ice-cream cone, and with a few rum-soaked raisins in the bottom for bait, the pheasants were easy to catch. They would place their beaks into the cone, and their feathers would stick to the honey. Because they could no longer see, they would stand absolutely still, so we could just walk through the wood, collecting them. Unless the cone came off, the birds were calm.

Another way to catch pheasants was to thread horsehair through currants. The birds would swallow the currant, and the hair would make it stick in its throat and all we had to do was follow the squawking itchy cough until the bird was in sight. Ivan also helped me make my own traps from wood and boxes, and I used them for wood pigeons as well as pheasants.

On days when the traps were out, we would go back after dark, collecting first the rabbits we had caught, and then once again for the empty ones. Whatever we went after, we would bag, it was easier to carry, and I didn't much like looking at the animals we had caught. I knew they would soon become food, but even so, I didn't like thinking about the transition from trap to plate.

Sometimes, though not often, Ivan would fancy some fish, or someone would ask him for fish, so he would take me down to the pond, and we would pour some lime into the water. This would soak up the oxygen, and after a while the fish would come to the surface, gasping for air. It was then just a matter of grabbing the fish and getting them home.

Ivan's style of fishing was indiscriminate, whatever fish happened to be around, it would eventually come up for air. Whereas I preferred fishing the way my father had taught me. Depending on the type of bait, and how and where I positioned myself, I could choose what I wanted to catch. I would fish for trout, but with a rod and bait, not the way Ivan had explained; I must have been too clumsy for fish tickling. He told me, that the trout is a curious fish, so when you leave a finger dangling in the water, it will glide by to investigate. All you have to do is stroke its belly gently, and like a puppy, the fish turns over and you just scoop it up into the net.

Most often I would go night-fishing with my friends on Fridays, because the following day wasn't a school day. That didn't matter to me, but I tried to be considerate to those who wanted to join me. Gary was a great friend; we used to go into the wood and build tree houses, and we used to set up tracks to follow on our bikes. The tracks usually included jumps. Before it got dark, we would set up camp, and get a fire going. Ivan had taught me how to clean up after myself, not just so no-one would recognise where I had been, but also because it was dangerous to leave human rubbish around the animals' domain.

Probably the most important thing I could have learnt while poaching and hunting was that humans are merely guests and must not disrupt the natural environment of the animal. Nature allows for human appetites and we are a part of the food chain, but as Ivan would tell me over and over again, we must never abuse what is around us.

These fishing trips with my friends allowed me to escape what was going on at home, and it gave me the opportunity to interact with my peers. That interaction was probably the only thing I missed by wagging school. On one fishing trip, my friend Mark and I were having a slow day. For hours we sat there and nothing was happening. Just when Mark was ready to give up, my hook caught on something. I tugged and the line was pulled taut. I tugged a bit harder, and out of the water a pack of four cans of beer swung in front of me.

When we weren't fishing, we would get up to all sorts of things; one of our favourites was to take some wool, and thread it through all the door knockers down the street last thing at night. So as the first car would pass through, it would set off all the knockers, and in an instant there would be at least a dozen confused and sleepy faces standing at the doors. We laughed and laughed until our sides ached, almost as much as we would ache after the beating we would get from Bob for annoying so many people.

We played all the usual games, like tag and chase, for which we didn't need anything, as well as various ball games. Kerby was something of a daily occurrence. We would all stand in line by the kerb, and each one of us would take the ball in turn, to throw it against the kerb until it stopped bouncing back, and then the next one would take over. This meant we were often all standing in the middle of the road, all the others acting as referees to the one playing, so after the third or fourth warning from an adult, the police would show up to clear the road. I know the adults didn't want to be scraping us off the road, but at the time, all I could see then, was that we weren't allowed to play our game.

Keresley End is a small place, and it didn't take long for the farmers to work out I was poaching, but I managed to keep out of their way. The farmers would set up traps for the foxes, and whenever I saw them, I would pull the snares. I liked to observe foxes, especially when they had cubs with them. To me they seemed like a stable family unit.

My sense of time was, and to some extent still is, distorted. I don't know how long I knew Ivan before he was too ill to go out, but he would still advise me when I went out by myself. He was going in and out of hospital; I would go to the caravan and call for him, but the only answer I would get would be from the animals. I'm not sure when he died, or what had caused his death, but one day he left for the hospital and never came back.

But before then, he took me hunting on a few occasions. I turned out to be quite a good shot. I remember watching Ivan holding the shotgun, explaining all the parts, showing me how to take it apart and put it back together again. While he was telling me why it is so important to keep each and every part clean, I was itching to get my hands on it. I wanted to try it out.

Of course I was aware that it was dangerous, and that it wasn't a toy, but it was the most exciting thing I had been allowed to use. It was loud and powerful, and it gave me the opportunity to have a sense of pride in myself. Looking back now, I realise that feeling of achievement and self-pride had nothing whatsoever to do with a weapon. It was all down to Ivan and the way he interacted with me. Even if he had taught me algebra, I think he would have created the same sorts of feelings, because he believed in me, and he believed I was capable.

We would leave the caravan just before dawn, and head out onto Corley Moor. It was funny, just as my eyes were adjusting to the low light, it would start to get brighter. So depending on what was on the menu, or what was about, and usually it was the latter, we would hunt either wood pigeons or rabbits. Sometimes we were lucky enough to bring back a deer, but most often it was something smaller and easier to carry.

Night-time was another thing altogether. Often we would go lamping. We used a really powerful torch or light and from one end of a field to the other, all the eyes would reflect back at us. In time I learnt to recognise the animals by the colour of their eyes. Rabbits would seem white, and foxes would be yellow in the bright light. The only problem was that cats' eyes would also shine white, so until you came up a little closer it was impossible to say which it was.

At night, the place looks like a completely different world. There are so many more animals about, birds, game, the odd stray from a local farm. I have to admit I tried to appease Bob by bringing back a chicken or two, but to no avail. Even stealing eggs and the odd duck didn't help. Even though I was making an effort to provide food for the table, either by bringing it back, or selling it on so we could buy things, my mother and stepfather didn't appreciate it. Most farmers didn't mind if you picked a handful from each crop, but they would obviously get angry if we abused the land and what they had grown.

So anything that came into sight became a target, and if I were successful, it would end up on my plate. Some nights, all I could manage would be half a dozen potatoes, but they would fill an empty stomach. On the days where I had to go out hungry, I had even more of an incentive to succeed. Each trip would take three to four hours, and because I slept so badly, I didn't have a sleep pattern to disrupt; I would just make up for the time later. Most often we wouldn't go more than five miles out, but now and again someone would offer to take us out a little further in a car. This was never very successful, probably because we knew our own territory, and we would rush because of the time we lost.

It was a good way to interact with others, and to some extent I had even managed to get a little envious respect from some of the older poachers when they saw how fast I was, and how accurate I was. There was one man, Stewart I think his name was who used a catapult. He taught me how to use it, and within weeks, I was stopping birds in flight.

The local bobby knew exactly what we were doing, but by the time I was going out with just my friends, he could neither catch us, nor prove we were up to anything. He would watch us, following our every move, but could never work out how to find the evidence he needed. Perhaps it was just the usual belief that anyone of school age out and about must be up to something, because no matter how many times he stopped to talk to us, he never accused us of anything specific.

What I did was for food, not for fun, or to satisfy some sort of bloodlust. I was taught well, and I learnt quickly because of necessity. Within months I was able to go out and return with food most nights, and it didn't matter whether I was using a shotgun or coursing dogs, or even ferrets. I also used traps and snares.

I kept my four ferrets in the old aviary at the back of the house. I would take them poaching one at a time, and they would be itching to get into a warren as soon as they could smell it. Ferrets usually go straight for the eyes, so they do not leave a lot of mess behind them. I trained them to return to a whistle, and because they associated whistling with food, they always returned, leaving the rabbit for me to dig out.

One early morning, my friends and I were coming back from a failed session; we had absolutely nothing with us, and I started telling them they must be jinxed, because I always bring something home. They laughed at me, and one of them said – well if you're so lucky, why don't you go and pick up that clump of grass, you'll find a rabbit underneath it. So I walked over and picked it up. It turned out to be a dead end of a warren, and sitting there, was a rabbit. I picked him up, and grinned. The others were stunned. Because we determined this was not very sporting of us, we let the rabbit go.

In the right hands, and with enough salt, herbs and spices, anything we were able to catch would become edible. A ten-year-old, eager to achieve as well as please, doesn't think to bring all the ingredients that make food a meal, so when we ate on the hoof, so to speak, we had to roast it over a fire, which often meant it would drop into the fire and *en croute* would actually be *en ash*. Either way, it was absolutely awful.

Ivan was brilliant when it came to food outside. He taught me to recognise wild herbs, and how to find them. He also explained that Nature knows best about food combinations because you will find they grow near to one another. Most of what we caught we would prepare at home, but sometimes, especially if we had time, he would put together a dish that tasted so good you would always want more. Once we were back home, we could also relax a little, so we could give our meal some thought.

Ivan was very particular about the rules of hunting and poaching. Anything you catch will be served on a plate. Brenda had no qualms about putting a rabbit or a pheasant in the oven, but some of the other things we caught, we knew we would have to eat ourselves. Some things we didn't even bother asking if anyone else would eat. Squirrel meat, as an example, is not something you crave, or enjoy for that matter. Perhaps one of our renowned TV chefs would make it appealing and tasty, yet I can't help but see a roasted rat on a bad hair day. If they tasted any better perhaps they would be extinct rather than endangered.

Another thing I didn't really take to when I prepared it myself was hedgehog. Once wrapped in clay, it could be baked in the fire until the clay hardens, and then the meat is ready too. As the clay is broken and separated from the hedgehog, the spikes remain in the clay, so it is just a matter of serving. The meat has a rich gamey taste, but there is only enough for a starter or a snack. It's simple, if you can recognise clay in its natural form. I gave up trying after a couple of attempts of using what I thought was clay. It would bake, but the heat wouldn't get through to the meat. I left baking to the experts.

One time I can remember going out and, I think my friend Johnny was with me, I spotted a rabbit about one hundred and fifty yards in front of me. I aimed, seeing the rabbit's face in my sight, and fired. I had used a single shot in a cartridge, in a 4-10 shotgun. The rabbit seemed startled, and from where we were standing it looked as if it had passed out. Getting closer to it, we realised I had shot it between the eyes. There was a round hole at the front, about the size of a peanut, but most of the back of the skull was missing.

Poaching was a nightly occurrence in our village, and most of the people I knew were involved. We used signals to let each other know it was safe to pass. We never fought over territory, but it was useful to know the figure walking towards you is not a farmer. On a few occasions I would be chased, but with all the training I did with Bob and his coal, I was never caught; at least, not red-handed. I was stopped once, but I was with some mates, and we managed to stow away what we had with us, so we were just strolling, minding our own business. They must have known, but we were kids, and without evidence, there was nothing they could do.

When I was with my friends, I was most often with Tim; it seems like I've known him forever. Well, any time we fancied going exploring, we would usually end up at the cliffs of Corley Rock. There were two sheer sides, which were also known as the Witches' Faces - the Midlands equivalent of the American Mount Rushmore. Because it is sandstone, it changes almost daily. Every time I go back to it I can see changes; I know when I first explored on Corley Rock it looked very different to the way it does now. A cave has appeared since, and when I look at the cliffs now I feel that I must have been mad to attempt climbing them.

I must have been inquisitive, but as there was no-one to explain things to me, I would try to work it all out myself. Camping underground was one thing that took me a long time to work out. The first time, we dug a tunnel, but we hadn't gone deep enough for the ground above us not to fall through. I had seen somewhere how they had built the trenches during the First World War, so I told the others and we went looking for things that would hold the roof up. After several attempts, we managed to make ourselves a living space no-one would spot. It was well supported, large enough for us to sleep in, and hidden to all who didn't know where it was

One summer, it must have been around the time Brenda told us Bob was going to marry her, I was most often at the ponds. So we were all there, Derby, Ian, Wally, busy doing nothing in particular, when someone had the brilliant idea that we should have a diving competition. We all took it in turns to climb the tree, and we all jumped to the left, hit the water and came out. That was until Derby got to the end of the branch. He dived to the right, and landed waist deep in the mud. This would have been funny had he been the right way up, slurping his way out to the bank. Instead he flew in head first, and all we could see was a pair of legs wriggling out of the water as if they were antennae on the top of some creature's head. He pulled himself out and just stood there waiting politely for us all to stop laughing hysterically.

I did anything and everything possible to escape what was going on in my mind. At home there seemed very little approval or praise for anything I did, so any self-confidence I should have had was worn away by the silence in between the criticism and beatings.

I realised there was nothing I could do to change what was happening. I tried stealing; Bob wasn't satisfied with the amount of coal I carried for him. I brought back game, and Brenda would moan she didn't have a clue what to do with an animal, she was used to cooking with meat. No matter what I did I would be beaten for it, and the only way I could fight back was to get lippy. As quickly as the sarcastic insults flew, so did the slaps and punches. I was too scared to defend myself because I wasn't aware of my own strength, so I would try to keep out the house and I'd be doing something simple like kicking a ball, and instead of thudding against a window, it would go straight through. At Halloween, when all my friends were staining windows and doors with eggs, my attempts would fly straight through, leaving a perfect circular hole in the pane. If I had carried on much longer, I think I would have been given a discount at the local glaziers. I almost expected them to provide an advertising sticker... as replaced by Roy.

Chapter Six

Fighting Back

B OB didn't like anyone to question his authority. As I grew bigger and stronger, I also grew braver. At first it was hardly noticeable; a quiet rumble of discontent climbing from the bottomless pit of anger inside me, until I could taste the hatred in my mouth. The first manifestation was mere defiance.

I didn't know which was worse, trying to get through the day without being stopped with blind panic and fear, or the nights, which would drag on for ever, allowing me not a minute's peace to rest; my mind forcing itself to comprehend what I had been through by playing the memories over and over again.

What Ison had put me through was bad enough the first time around. It was traumatising; I wasn't able to forget it for a second. Although my memory is vague when it comes to other things, the abuse I was subjected to, has been branded onto my memory with such clarity that it is at times difficult to see it is only a memory, and that it is not happening again.

As well as my brain taunting me incessantly, I was trying to find ways of avoiding Bob, as well as anything else that may set off a flashback. I didn't realise at the time what they were; it was yet another thing I wanted to escape. Ivan was a help; the way he talked to me was a distraction from my own thoughts, and he allowed me to use my imagination in a good way. He showed me that hope and optimism are necessary in getting through the day.

Nan Hutchings was someone I could rely on for support; I never told her what happened. Once Brenda had refused to listen, I couldn't expect anyone else to. Instinctively she knew something was wrong, but Nan never put any pressure on me to say anything by asking. She would let me do all the talking, and she would listen sympathetically, even when I couldn't find the words to express what I was trying to say.

I was so self-centred and obsessed with fighting my past, I'm surprised I had noticed anything at all. But Nan wasn't behaving the way she should. It was silly things at first. She did all the things she had done before, like cooking and baking. She would tell me stories about the past, though she had never been one to divulge much about the family's skeletons, but she started using a fork to put sugar in her tea. She would tell me about the things she did in her childhood, as if it had happened just a few days ago. Nan would put something down next to her, and then search the whole house for it, forgetting what she was looking for. It must have been a scary time for her; I think she was too proud to admit anything was wrong, so she would try to hide it.

I tried telling Brenda that Nan wasn't behaving the way she used to, but, Brenda being Brenda, she just ignored me, and if she noticed anything herself, she would have hoped it would sort itself out without her having to do anything about it. I watched Nan get worse and worse, not knowing what I could do to help, when the only person who I could turn to for help, had ignored me once again. It seemed to go on for such a long time, but for all I know it may have only been weeks.

The doctor was finally called in, and he told us that she had suffered several strokes, one after the other. Without tests, it would be impossible to determine how many there had been. They took her to hospital, and I can remember visiting her, but she would have no idea who I was. I knew that was because she was ill, but it still hurt. This was another thing that managed to put a distance between me and those I wished I could be close to.

It was the same with Ivan. I wanted both of them to be proud of me; I didn't want them to think they had wasted their time and attention for nothing. I wanted them to know I would make the effort because they deserved that much from me. At least Ivan and Nan Hutchings, more than anyone else thus far, merited seeing me succeed.

Nan was in the hospital bed, surrounded by what looked like hundreds of tubes and wires; she seemed to be shrinking under the weight of them. Bob and Brenda were there, and one of my aunts also. Ian and I were also crowding the room. Nan had become so weak and frail that her skin seemed stretched and see-through. She was colourless, almost translucent and so still. I had to listen carefully for her breath above the noise of all the machines, and the clock seemed louder and louder, until I thought I wouldn't hear anything else.

The adults were talking amongst themselves; no-one noticed Nan had tried to move. Without warning, like an air-raid siren, the alarm bells rang out. As if they had been standing outside waiting, the doctor and nurses rushed in, their hands like a blur. We were pushed out of the way, or maybe we just pushed past each other to clear the way. It all went quiet. Even before anyone had the time to see, I knew I was on my own.

Back at home, nothing had changed; much like before, Bob would be standing in front of me, fist lifted to shoulder height and, without realising this time, I mumbled something. It was so quiet, even I hadn't heard what I said. I know I didn't swear; I didn't dare, not even in my thoughts. He stopped, so surprised that the fist fell open, and then the realisation of what had happened, and wham!

Once again I was on the floor, counting stars. It didn't matter that much, because I had stepped over the line and survived. Each time it would become easier and easier to confront my demons, when I had just proved to myself I was brave enough to face Bob.

Our next-door neighbour used to moan all the time. It was never anything important, just a continuous high-pitched drone of complaint about nothing. So one day I had this great idea that would make him either get annoyed or shut him up. He grew onions in his back garden, and they had pride of place. All lined up neatly, growing parallel to each other, the shoots standing proud and green above the ground. Perhaps I should explain that he would moan at all the children at least a dozen times a day, just for playing. I thought he should feel what he put us through, and I thought I could make him understand. Derby was with me, and he's the proverbial bull. He'll have an idea, and then the brain switches off, until he's finished. Derby is not the sort of guy who doesn't follow through. I can't remember now whose idea it was, but between us we decided to turn his onions upside down.

We had done a job to be proud of. We were neat and tidy, and we were quiet. Moany Ernie woke up to a beautiful sunny morning, opened his curtains to stare lovingly at his prize crop, when all he could see was the scraggly roots sitting on top. 'Oh Goodness!' he said. 'That must have been that little angel from next door.' Or at least that's what I thought I heard in amongst the four-letter words that echoed down the street. If you hadn't already guessed, my backside was as blue as the air next door.

So was my back. Bob chased me into the back garden, but before I heard his almost lumbering gait and thumping footsteps behind me, something heavy crashed into the middle of my back, and I fell to the ground under the weight. I turned around, and saw that Bob had thrown half a paving slab at me. The bruise seemed to grow from the back to my front; I just ached for days, I couldn't move at all for three of them. If I had stood still to take my punishment, maybe he would have stopped with the beating. But I showed him that he didn't matter to me - his beatings were nothing. He couldn't cope with that sort of insubordination, so he threw the first thing he could get hold of.

I was always getting into trouble for anything that involved next door. Brenda hated the thought that anyone might disapprove. What other people thought was important, because Brenda's whole world revolved around their comments and opinions. Like the time I got sick of the old lady staring at me from the upstairs window. She was most likely a lovely woman; I just didn't want her spying on me. She used to sit in a rocking chair and as she came forward, all you could see was an old withered and white face in the window. I felt uncomfortable, due to unwanted contact with others, and I wasn't yet ready to deal with that. So I got a paintbrush and some black paint, and all the windows disappeared by morning. Brenda didn't ask me why I did it; her comment was along the lines of, 'now what will these people think of me, letting you do something like that.'

There were days when I would mope, trying not to do anything, forcing myself to remember good days, so I could persuade myself that, by the end of my life, there would be more good days than bad. I would stop to think about Ivan and how he used to explain things to me, and I would listen, grateful for the positive attention. He made learning a thrill; it was exhilarating watching something happen the way he said it would. On just such a day I got to thinking about how a gun fires its bullet, and I wondered if I could make that happen myself. I thought it all through, how to build up the pressure, how to create the right temperature, carefully choosing what I would need for my experiment.

I got a piece of copper tubing, about two feet long, and I stuffed it with cotton wool, pressing it tight. I then opened up a cartridge, and removed everything and placed it into the copper tube as I had found it, so wadding first, the gunpowder, then the shots, and finally some more wadding. I then placed it into the fire, not really expecting anything to happen. I watched it for about ten minutes, and then decided I had forgotten something, and I got lost in my own thoughts, trying to work out where I had gone wrong. Perhaps another five minutes later, a huge explosion brought me back from my calculations.

Because I had used copper, which heats evenly but slowly, the length I had used needed about fifteen minutes to reach the temperature needed to set it off. The whole room was filled with thick black smoke, and as my eyes and ears adjusted to what had just happened, I noticed Ian sitting up on the sofa where he had been dozing. Inches above his head were feathers from the pillow and black stains from the burning cotton wool. He was incoherent, from sleep or maybe from shock, but I'm sure the stream of bad language implied he had no idea what had happened.

From the force of the gunpowder, the pipe struck into the back of the fireplace, shaking everything in the chimney, and clearing the flue. Everything else flew out and towards Ian. We were so lucky, it would have taken mere millimetres in any direction and I could have been looking at a murder charge. Now, Brenda and Bob were upstairs at the time, and I thought there was no way I could escape a beating; this time it may be the last. Brenda came down by herself to see what was going on.

She told us to clean up before Bob woke up. I couldn't believe what she was saying; Bob was still asleep. He hadn't heard a thing. He was at the back of the house, and slept right through. Moany Ernie on the other hand heard it and was at our door to see what we were doing, even before Brenda came downstairs. It wasn't until then that I realised that when Bob was on the night shift, Brenda would prepare the back room for him so they wouldn't disturb each other with their syncopated sleep patterns. She must have had her reasons to keep out of his way as much as we did. I just didn't want to see it.

Some mornings, the whole family would climb shakily down the stairs with a familiar hobble; it was obvious it hurt us all to breathe. It wasn't that I didn't notice; it didn't interest me, because I was preoccupied with what had happened to me and what I was going through, so that it took some time to register with me that Bob was also beating Brenda. When I started to ask her why she was bruised, she would tell me she had hit her eye/her nose/her cheek/or whichever part of her body was bruised on the bedside table. Not once did I believe her. For one thing, just like most of my bruises, they were the same size and shape as Bob's fist.

I didn't like what Bob was doing to my mother, but I wasn't going to fight her battles when I had so many of my own to contend with. In any case, she was an adult; she knew what to do in a situation like that. It never occurred to me that she might be too scared to do anything. It didn't occur to me either that she might have just accepted what was going on because she wasn't willing to lose the relationship. I always believed adults have the power of choice. They do things because they choose to. Only children have to do what others tell them to. As I grew up, I found out age and size have nothing to do with choice.

In retrospect, I can tell Brenda became withdrawn and quiet. She seemed interested only in when and where her next drink and cigarettes were coming from. Even more than before, she was cold towards us; I can't imagine if we made her feel guilty or if she blamed us in some way. Perhaps she thought that, had Ian and I been better behaved, Bob would have been a better husband to her. However she coped, and whatever she was thinking, Lucy was always by her side and on her side. Still, mother and daughter are very close. Although I do not envy Lucy's relationship with Brenda, I think it just made me more aware of what I was missing. It would have been all too easy to take the blame, but as I grew up, I knew all I could do was forgive if and when I had the strength to do so.

The only time Bob didn't go out drinking was when he was working nights. Brenda would normally join him, that is when she didn't go to the bingo hall. They would head off to the Coventry Colliery Club, because apart from the Golden Eagle, it was one of the very few places in Keresley End where they could get a drink.

I on the other hand had found two outlets for my feelings. The first was very physical and aggressive - it was noticeable from the start - whereas the other, even I didn't realise, was a coping mechanism. The physical was symbolic, I ran as much as possible, and as often as I could. I knew I would never be able to escape what was going on in my head; wherever I went I would take it with me, but the physical exhaustion from running gave me a sense of relief. I also began fighting; I needed to find a way of showing others around me what I was feeling. Any time I tried to tell them, when I tried to explain, I was ignored or even worse, ridiculed.

One day I got so upset, and now I don't even remember what it was about, but I know the frustration built up until I felt such an enormous pressure, I swung around to see my fist make contact with the wall. As I pulled it away, I saw the dent my knuckle had made. Unlike Bob, I was going to make a conscious effort to control my temper.

Whilst fishing, I would take a pencil and paper with me, and I would sketch what I had caught. This was something I used to do most often when I was alone, especially as I would get angry with myself if my drawing didn't look anything like the catch. With plenty of practice, I started to draw other things as well. Later on I could recognise how I was feeling at the time of each drawing by the colours I had used. The reds and oranges betrayed my anger, and blue showed the world my isolation. Not that anyone took any notice of it. I suppose Bob was glad that I had found something to keep me quiet and out of the way. As long as it didn't interfere with his coal distribution, he couldn't have cared less how it made me feel.

I was noticing improvements in my art, and it felt like an accomplishment. Soon the subjects changed and I was drawing animals such as tigers and elephants from photographs and at the zoo, although I didn't go all that often. I liked watching a picture come about. It's a bit like the dot of light in the middle of the television screen just after you have switched it off, but in reverse. With a drawing you start with a dot, or a point of focus, and the image builds around it.

I pushed myself harder and harder in my running also, so that every time I managed a better time, I knew I had a reason to be proud of myself. I think if I had had the support I wanted in the first place, I would never have pushed myself so hard and so far. When you're self-taught, you soon realise how bad a pupil you are; you tend to focus on the negative. Perhaps it was just me; I had very little positive feedback, so I was more inclined to see what was wrong, rather than what was right. With time - I suppose everything takes practice - I learnt to be more objective, and once I had passed that obstacle, it was easier for me to see that I was making progress.

It was very much a one-step-forward and two-steps-back sort of journey. Each flashback could set me back so far that it would seem I had never started. I could never be sure what would set them off, but smells seemed to cause the most realistic ones. I could be in a room full of people and I would be completely alone except for the delicate yet very real feeling of a shiver crawling over my skin. However obscure, my brain would form a link of associations that would all inevitably return to the same thing. Waiting for a bus, and someone walks by in a pair of smart black trousers – Ison's friend used to wear the same style, and would visit when Ison was sitting with us; when he goes, Ison would start with me. My brain thinks it's a danger. I see a cat sitting on a fence, it turns towards me, and it seems the cat looks at me accusingly.

I go to the shop to get Bob a newspaper, and the rows and rows of chocolate and sweets in plain view remind me how easy it is to persuade a small child to like you. I would walk past the house where Nan Hutchings used to live, and instead of remembering how much she loved me, all I would hear buzzing in my ears would be Brenda's voice telling me not to mention it ever again. A knock at the door, and all the hairs on my body stand on end; I'm ready to escape whoever it is. So each minute would pass with me trying to overcome my obstacles, both real and imagined. I say imagined, but my mind would torture me in a much worse manner than Bob's beatings could.

The running helped me escape Bob's temper at least. As I got faster, I became more comfortable with it, so I had more of an incentive to continue. One afternoon, a P.E. teacher spotted me outside the school, and gave chase. I did what was by now natural. I lost him in the distance behind me, when he realised he wouldn't be able to catch up. The next time he saw me, he suggested we could forget all about the previous incident if I was willing to join the cross-country team.

This teacher saw the raw potential of an untrained athlete. I saw an opportunity to prove to myself that I could amount to something. Bob and Brenda no longer seemed worth the effort. This teacher was proud of his talent-spotting, and I was glad there was someone around who would say, 'You did better this time', or 'Keep it up, and you'll improve soon.' He helped me train not just for cross-country running, but also marathons. I managed three, but as I had always preferred cross-country running I didn't take the marathon races seriously enough to continue training for them.

I seem to remember other teachers were not as enthusiastic about my presence. One incident springs to mind. I made the effort to get to school; I hoped the way the day at senior school was divided might mean I could cope a little easier with the lessons. But I was running late; Bob had made sure I was bruised and battered, and on top of all that I was also tired. I usually liked my geography classes, but for some reason - maybe she was on maternity leave - we had a substitute teacher, and on seeing me turn up late, looking as I did, he called me a tramp. All this within the first thirty seconds of me opening the door, and loud enough for the whole class to hear. Instead of taking his criticism with good grace, I threw a chair at him. He was later reprimanded for his behaviour; obviously someone among the staff had noticed things were not quite right with me.

Still looking for an escape, I took to swimming every day at the Coventry Baths, not only was it a good workout, it also helped me concentrate on something other than my own thoughts. Whenever I had an opportunity to focus on my body's functioning, I could, at least for a little while, think only of breathing in and out, seeing in my mind's eye the simple but relaxing, regular movement of my lungs; my brain aware of the body and nothing surrounding it. Up and down the pool, length after length, I was in my own world, away from the fears.

Like most of the streets in the country, Thompsons Road threw a party for the Queen's Jubilee in 1977. There was a disco on the playing field - everyone was there - and it must have gone on for longer than I expected. I was genuinely tired and willing to go to sleep. Bob was working so he was out the way, and I managed to relax a little. I even had fun. I can remember thinking how surprised I was that everyone was in high spirits.

Bob was getting more and more vicious with his punishments, probably out of spite. He hated the idea that one day soon I may stand up to him, and there won't be a thing he will be able to do about it. I had wagged from school for yet another day, and as I walked through the door, I caught sight of Bob holding the poker. It was only when I made eye contact that I realised it was for me. I turned around, by now I was so much faster than Bob that he didn't particularly try to chase after me. I knew he expected me to be back later, and that he would wait for me.

I decided to run away. I survived for about a week all by myself sleeping in a barn. It was warm in the hay, even if it was a little prickly. I had to pinch milk from doorsteps, and I ate raw eggs. Until I found a box of matches, I only had the choice of cold and raw. The matches meant I could start a fire. I found a loaf of bread outside one of the local shops, and I made myself some toast. That was the best meal I'd had in what seemed like a long time. I was aware I was gone from home for only a few days, and I ate whenever I could, but I think that toast tasted so good because it was proof of victory. I didn't need butter to make a perfect breakfast; it was the knowledge that I was capable enough to survive on my own.

I wasn't strictly on my own; Ian joined me, as did my friend Mark. Within two days, Ian had had enough, and a couple of days after that, Mark went home as well. With Ian being back at home, he would sneak food out to us, so we wouldn't risk getting caught by stealing. I would wait for him at the club, and we would chat for a while, usually about nothing in particular.

We slept in the hay, and one morning I heard voices around, so I covered myself up completely and I stayed hidden until they went away. We had escaped capture; we were so, so proud of ourselves. All that day we were on top of the world, strutting like peacocks in our own imaginations. By the second day on my own, Ian was trying desperately to get me to go back home. He even promised me that Bob had told him if I came home I wouldn't be beaten. I don't believe Ian intentionally lied to me, but the worst mistake I made was to go back.

I also started to rebel more than ever; it seemed only fair that if I was going to get into trouble anyway, I may as well find something to fit the punishment. I was known to the police; I was one the kids they wanted to 'keep an eye on' otherwise they were sure I'd go astray. Bob would take us more or less nightly to the pit, so it was inevitable that we would be caught once or twice; sometimes we would get a verbal clip 'round the ear' for being there, and then again from Bob, for getting noticed. Most of what I got up to was trivial, kids' stuff; even the police wouldn't take it further, but there were times when I overstepped the mark, and had to appear before the court.

Chapter Seven

Making My Way

I MUST have been about eleven when I first started working. Ivan got me a job helping out with the cleaning on a farm nearby. It was smelly, hard, and tiring work. Yet I enjoyed every minute of it. It got me away from the house, so I wasn't in Bob's way. It kept me busy, so my mind didn't have the chance to wander as it did usually.

I didn't escape the flashbacks entirely, but at the same time I wasn't in that heightened sense of danger all the time. At first I would be mucking out the sties. I can remember my first promotion. I was so proud I was being given more responsibility. It proved to me that the farmer believed I was capable. The transition between the pig sty and the cow shed was simple. I was doing the same work, but there was just more of it. In time I got to clean out the stables as well. I was so glad this farmer didn't keep elephants!

I used to go to the farm first thing in the morning, and I would finish my usual chores before the school day started, if I was in the mood for it. Although most often, I just wanted to be alone. More and more I would take my sketch book with me, and draw what was around me. The farm animals humoured me, posing for the drawing, until they got bored waiting for me to get it right. Once I got home, I would use those sketches and repeat the drawing, not just for the practice, but also to rectify mistakes. Within months I was doing less at home, and more from sight.

By the time I got onto the YTS scheme to work on that same farm, I had learnt to drive the tractor. I was paid sixteen pounds a week and I had to prove I was committed to the trade, and that I would be willing to complete the apprenticeship. I had no trouble getting accepted; after all I had five years to prove myself. During crop picking, I would take the tractor out to the fields, where the pickers would pile the crop into the back, and I would drive back to the storehouse.

In the meantime, I managed to make one mistake after another, or perhaps I should call them setbacks. About a month after I had made my escape from Bob, and my subsequent return, I had found a wallet in the car park by the club. My friend Brian Hobbs was with me. We were more impressed that we had found it than the fact that it was full. That thought occurred to us on the way home. As we had no idea as to how we could return it, I decided to give it to Bob. Brian came with me, because he had been there when I found it. I thought he could help me explain better. Bob didn't want to hear what either of us had to say. He just assumed I had stolen it. It was personal property, and even the man who had taught me to steal coal from the pit had some morals and standards.

'This was wrong', he raved at me as his fist landed bang in the middle of my face. My nose felt as if it had been pushed into my skull. I stood there crying so hard that if my nose hadn't been bleeding I'm sure it would have been running. Brian must have been glad when Bob suggested to him that he should go home. Once he heard the front door click shut, Bob really laid into me. I spent the next three days in bed. Had I been put through a meat grinder I couldn't have felt any worse. On the fourth day I only hobbled out of bed to escape a nightmare.

This incident gave Brenda the strength to tell Bob that if we needed chastising, she would be responsible for it. She would then take us upstairs and beat the mattress instead of either Ian or me. This proved to me how scared she was of Bob, and the reality of his doing serious damage to us.

It took us a while to realise it, but Brenda had started seeing someone else. I can remember talking to Ian about it, hoping that she would make a clean break and take us with her. Our hopes were raised when we saw she was getting more and more involved. We kept praying she would leave Bob; I didn't care whom she was having an affair with - no-one could be any worse. For some reason it just petered out, and Brenda stayed with her husband. Ian and I would have to make our own escape.

A little later I decided I should try to find my dad. I found out that once we had moved out, he kept lodgers, but moved away soon after. Brian Hobbs was with me; in fact it was his dad who managed to trace the whereabouts of my father. It took a long time for us to find him, and when we went to visit, the journey was a long one. We had to get a bus into

Coventry, and then we headed out to Wood End. It was such an anti-climax when I finally saw him again.

He just didn't want to know. At least that was the impression he left with me. He couldn't look me in the eye; he had nothing to say to me. He showed no feelings towards me; it was as if I was no relation to him. Although looking back as an adult I don't know how he would have managed with a child and working and everything else he would have had to do. Even so it must have been difficult not seeing his children any more. I don't know if he felt he needed to justify why he made no contact, or if he thought I wanted something from him as compensation. This, guilt I suppose you could call it, I carry around with me to this day. I can only think that he felt abandoned. Perhaps it was easier for him to cope by severing all contact. As an adult I have seen him on just a few occasions around Coventry, and quite by chance. But what hurts me most of all is when he calls me Ian. After all I was named after him.

It was difficult having to deal with physical pain, rejection from both my parents, fear created by my own memories, the fear anticipated by my heightened and oversensitive understanding of danger, bullying at school because it was so obvious I was an outsider and a loner, and then on top of all that, injustice.

It might sound melodramatic, but I genuinely was in the wrong place at the wrong time. On previous occasions I didn't think to lie, so if I were caught doing something I shouldn't, I admitted it. I was used to Bob dishing it out generously, so I assumed it was the same at the courts. As a juvenile, there is only so much they can do. After all, it had been years since they had sent anyone to Australia, although that would have been a sufficient distance away from Bob and Ison.

Things got serious when I was brought before the court for breaking into the local ATC centre. That would not have been too bad by itself, except it wasn't me. Or should I say it wasn't us. Ian was blamed as much as I was. It turned out to be serious because they found us at the scene of the crime. The actual break-in happened about two days before, and it was done by some boys from Bedworth, not that this vague information could be of any use to me. And I only found out when they read the charges to us that firearms had been stolen. So there I stood, in that lifeless court, dressed smart, trying to stand tall, but managing to slouch nervously anyway. Three pairs of piercing and accusing eyes stared without blinking, trying to understand why I would do such a thing, and with a history like mine, tut

tut tut. It didn't help that I was known to the bench. Even though I knew they had a set choice of punishments they could give us, my worst fear was they would decide to let Bob deal with me. Coming from such a small place, most people seemed to know I went poaching; they knew Bob took us to the pit, so what else were they to assume? Ian and I were the oldest, so we got the severest of punishments. I was given a four-month detention centre order.

What had actually happened, was Derby, Ian and I, along with the rest of the gang, went by, and we saw the ATC centre was broken into. I stood outside, while some of the others had gone in to see what was in there. They brought out the safe because they couldn't open it. It took me maybe five minutes; I must have been working instinctively. It was as if I had a subconscious understanding of the mechanism. In any other circumstances I would never have attempted it, but friends have a way of getting you involved.

While in the detention centre, I met a boy who was there because he had shot his father through a hedge. He said it was all an accident, but I did wonder. He asked me to help him get out. The conversation ran a bit like the scenes from all those prison movies I had seen; we discussed our options huddled into corners, nothing said louder than a whisper. In the end he thought the best way to escape would be to get to the infirmary. We needed to cause an injury serious enough to get him hospitalised, but we didn't want to do any permanent damage. In the end we decided to break his leg, by using a fire extinguisher. He managed to get away, but I never found out if we broke the bone or not.

The detention centre was run like a boot camp; the simplest way to describe it would be Bergen-Belsen with regular meals. If anyone had made a mistake, we would all be punished. It was hard work, but I soon realised I was safe, and I would have somewhere to sleep, and I would be fed three times a day. The centre was organised into common rooms and individual cells, I would imagine like its adult counterpart. Each cell was no more than eight feet by six. There was a single bed, and a small cupboard, and we all had a window looking out onto a field. The place would get very claustrophobic for me; even in the large common rooms I needed my space. I'm not sure if having a view of an open rolling field helped or made things worse for me. That sentence was probably the biggest deterrent they could have used.

What helped was the fact that one of the first people we met on arrival was a Mr Jones. He was a large man, even bigger than Bob, loud and aggressive. He was Welsh and oppressive. Ian showed he wasn't afraid of anyone by shooting his mouth off. I was too tired to do anything; I just wanted to sleep. Ian was getting reprimanded, and then it became physical. I could see where it was going; I had seen it so many times with Bob. When I started laughing, I too got a slap. Jones seemed like a violent man, someone who enjoyed having power. Soon enough he proved himself to be a kitten, willing to laugh and talk with any of us. It wasn't all an act; Jones was never a soft touch. He demanded respect and got it.

As I got to know the system, I discovered that if anyone was found dawdling it would mean we would all be punished for it. We had no hot, or even warm, water to shave with, and we had to wear a tie. The colour showed our station inside. Most of the inmates arrived alone and made friends quickly. Pairs of brothers were unusual at the detention centre, Ian and I being the second pair thus far, which made us memorable.

We were all given paid jobs, and the money we were given, we could spend in the heavily subsidised shop. One of the things we had to do was stripping copper. We were paid twenty-five pence for every ten kilograms, and it was heavy monotonous work that needed no thought whatsoever. Stripping copper was something that proved useful to me later, because I was one of very few who could do it by hand and quickly enough for there to be any profit from it. The top wage may not sound like a lot, but, on the inside, two pounds seventy-five a week was an absolute fortune. Some weeks, I even had some left over.

Because I was the oldest, and there were firearms involved, I was taken to court for a second time unlike the rest of the team. Most of the sentences were running concurrently, so they would finish at the same time, but I was sentenced to a further six months to be served in Youth Custody. I was expecting this change to be one for the worse. But I was seen as something of a hero because I had survived the Detention Centre.

The screws, usually very cold and distant, got talking to me on the way to the court. They must have noticed I was frightened by the fact that I was going to a Crown Court. It was more serious than I had imagined, and I wasn't willing to accept responsibility for someone else's mistakes. Once again I had no choice in the matter. The Court is not interested in how guilty the defendant is, the question is simply - guilty or not guilty? I should have been in handcuffs the whole time, but they allowed me some dignity while we were alone. They told me I was supposed to be handcuffed and watched, even if I wanted to use the toilet. They gave me the benefit of doubt, which was just enough for me to do as they asked. We stopped for a meal on the way back, and they even let me have a drink with them at what turned out to be the local.

I have to explain; the Detention Centre was in the middle of nowhere, on a moor with nothing else around for miles, except for Youth Custody, which was a part in the same building complex. So the local was miles away, but also the closest proof of society in the area. The pub stands out in my memory because of its name – *'who'd have thought of that?'* - original and apt. For miles and miles around there is just empty space, until you come across the pub.

Youth Custody was organised into dorms, and the staff let us find our own pecking order, by ignoring the fact that a Kangaroo Court was held on a regular basis. Much like what we had seen, we would imitate the real thing, and get away with punishments more severe, because we were all peers. Judges, jury, and the executioners, all equal to the defendant. Anyone unwilling to serve the punishment declared would be next in line. Usually the defendant would be hit with something, once by everyone else in his dorm. The screws would normally wake us up early the following morning, just to make sure we knew they were really in charge, and that the pecking order goes way above us.

Within two weeks I was promoted to making the teas and coffees, as well as the sandwiches for any of the meetings that went on while I was there. I got to meet all the governors and the regular visitors to both the Detention Centre and Youth Custody. I even had my own little office or room in the admin. block, where I had a sofa bed, and I was allowed to make the space my own. I basically had the run of the place, on condition that I was on standby with the kettle as and when necessary. The secretaries obviously took a liking to me, as they would often bring me a cream cake from the outside as a treat.

I was the perfect choice for running contraband, and it was in my interest to keep in the good books of the others, not just with the staff. I had the freedom to move around the grounds, within reason, but it meant I could get to the gates and smuggle for the others. It was usually jewellery, and I would have the difficult task of trying to remember what belonged to whom, and the message that came with it. It may have been pure chance, but more likely someone grassed, and the screws put me through a shakedown. I hadn't planned on living that close to the edge, so I was glad they didn't find anything. It is true, it is always in the last place you look, but the search was stopped short of the sugar and coffee canisters. I was safe for now, but I thought I should play it safe from then on. I didn't want to give them a reason to keep me there any longer than necessary.

While I was there, I continued running, and I was entered in a five-mile cross-country race. I managed to win, by about two laps faster than the previous record-holder. I was given a Mars bar for this achievement. It may not seem like much, but to me it proved chocolate is not just a bribe.

Once I was out, Bob used his connections at the pit to get me a job. I was up at the top, and I was happy working. Down below in the actual pit, it was darker than I could have ever imagined. It seemed to me like the darkness was thick and heavy as it closed in on you, smothering your eyes until you persuade yourself you had never been able to see at all. The darkness of the pit makes you vulnerable, not to others, but to yourself. The physical darkness allows you to look inside yourself and see the whole being with such clarity that it scares you that first time. I wasn't ready for that, so I stayed up on top in the processing area.

The work didn't scare me; I was often working sixteen-hour shifts. Sometimes when the others in the team would be slacking, I could still shift the coal they expected to be moved in the usual eight hours. What worked out quite nicely was that Bob was working in a different shift to me, so as I started work, he would be leaving the pit. By this time we would have verbal spats, and now and again it would get physical, but our normal greeting would be some cutting remark, oozing with bile.

Bob's best mate had been a man called Savage, but at some point they argued, and they could barely be civil. Savage was trying to do exactly the same as Bob, and get all his sons a job in the pit. Now there was a lad who was perhaps a couple of years younger than me, and was what we used to call a bit soft in the head. I found out later that he had suffered from Asperger's Syndrome. He would get picked on, sometimes for no reason at all. More often than not it would be one or another of Savage's sons who was trying to make him leave so all the Savages could work there. I couldn't bear it. The lad worked hard; he tried to be pleasant, and I didn't believe he deserved what the Savages were doing to him.

One day, already fit to burst with anger, I saw them in the changing room picking on the boy. I just stormed in, mouthed something vicious to Bob who was on his way out, and, fist thumping, I kept hitting Savage until I had pushed him through the changing room and into the shower and out on the other side.

Bob's sideline was, if you'll pardon the pun, a goldmine. We would get in, and start shovelling coal from the top of the pile. From there you could see the bingo hall, and the bus stop. More often than not, people would see me on the pile and shout out. 'Bring me two bags, Roy, and I'll see you right in the morning!' Even the security guards would put in orders for their coal.

One time, we thought we would take it easy and we used a van. It was just bad luck that the gaffer had swapped places with the security guard who had let us in, and he closed the gates. We drove around to the main gate, and they were locked too. Using the van was just blatant stealing, and we had to get out before we were noticed. We had no choice but to ram the gate to make our escape. After that, we went back to the old ways.

I changed jobs often, never settling into any one career. I had worked as a doffer at one point, putting yarns and threads onto bobbins for the weaving looms. That was probably the least physical job I had; I always preferred to be active, and if at all possible, outside. Pipe-laying for BP was fun, as was working with the council sewerage department. Several times I managed to burst a mains, not realising my own strength. It didn't help that I was also enthusiastic in my work, so sometimes I wasn't always concentrating on what I should be doing.

My friend Mark taught me everything I needed to know when it came to construction and building. On and off, we worked together for years. I was eager to learn, and he was happy to teach. Later on he also showed me some carpentry, all of which I knew would come in useful. From digging and constructing a foundation, to making and putting up a shelf.

Later on I liked driving, almost as much as I liked running. It had the same effect, but it also brought in a wage. It was the sort of job that allowed me to keep calm, and even if I couldn't control the flashbacks, I could at least cope with them a little easier.

Another job I enjoyed greatly was one of landscape gardening. I think I just got swept along. I helped out a few friends with their gardens, and word got out I wasn't too bad at it. I would receive phone calls which would start with, 'Are you the bloke who did so and so's garden?' I took pride in the fact that my efforts were appreciated by others. It was a nice feeling, once I had finished a job, to think someone will enjoy looking at my work day in, day out. Of course, gardens are living and never static, and within a week they're no longer as I had planned them. Some people would ask me to look after the upkeep of their garden. One man in particular wanted me to take over all his gardens. I assumed he meant front and back, but he didn't say both, he used the word all. I decided to double-check. He then went on to explain that he owned several houses, which he uses for his guests when they come to visit him.

When I went to see all eight houses to give him a quote, he told me he had a good memory so there would be no need for written invoices, and if I accepted the job, I should know he only works in cash. Although I never felt that I would get to know him, he came across as a distant yet professional man. I had a respect for his way of working. He was calm, straight-talking, punctual, and above all, polite. What I also liked with him was that he didn't interfere with my work; he accepted that as far as landscapes are concerned, I know more than he does, which is why he employed me.

Most of his houses seemed empty most of the time, but that could have been because he called me in to work just before and just after he had visitors. Letting my imagination run away with itself, I pondered what sort of business he was involved in, because not once did he mention what he did. I used to wonder who his associates were, as well. This gave me a chance to escape my demons even if I didn't have the strength to fight them.

One of my first jobs as an adult was that of road sweeper. I liked the job. I was with the council, which meant there was some security in it. I was in the job for about eighteen months when my temper got the better of me. The man who would tell us where we would be working each morning was the sort of fool so far up himself that he had no respect for anyone else. The whole world was beneath him, or at least his attitude made me think that.

He used to demand that things get done; he never once asked. He was arrogant and nasty with it. I kept quiet for as long as I could and then told him what everyone thought of him. He tried and succeeded in making my life hell there. I took the not so subtle hint and started looking for another job. Once I got the job with a window manufacturing company, I was free.

At the window company, I had an accident with a drill. I cut my hand, almost severing a finger. I was in hospital, and then I was given two weeks of sick leave. My sick pay was going to be given to me the same way my wages were paid. So instead of me going to the office to pick them up, Ian and my mates Fatman, Wally, and of course Derby, went to pick it up. It was close to Halloween Night, and because we were always playing practical jokes on each other, they decided to wear masks while collecting my sick pay.

The people in the office thought it was an armed robbery, and when they took their masks off, Derby and the others could tell immediately the office was suffering from a missing sense of humour. We all thought it was hilarious. And how I laughed... when I went to pick up my P45.

Chapter Eight

Some Light Relief

AS A CHILD I had friends who did some pretty stupid things. I'm not saying I was sensible, but, when I think back, we managed to escape death more or less once a week. And we were doing these things intentionally.

Picture Derby with his first love, a 125cc motorbike, riding around and around until he gets to a holly bush. Normal people go around bushes more than a foot high. Derby comes up to an eight-foot high holly bush, and doesn't even slow down. He must have thought sheer brute force would see him through. I wish I could describe the sound of hundreds of holly leaves piercing skin. The bike carried on all the way through, and Derby fell back on the other side of the bush. When he looked up, he could see his own imprint in the foliage, and a big gaping hole where the bike should have been.

Ian wasn't any better when it came to bikes either. One time he was riding around the wood, going as fast as he dared, and tried to go between two trees - except that he missed. I was in tears before he was, but I was crying with laughter. The trees stopped him, but the bike got away. I went over to him, his arms outstretched like Frankenstein. All he could say was, 'I think I broke 'em.' Then he passed out.

Then there was the time he forgot about a bend in the road and flew into the kerb. It was more like a bank, being two feet high. The bike stopped just short of the kerb, and Ian flew into the field behind it. He hit the mud as if it were concrete, then slowly sank into it.

For once I agreed with Bob when he finally decided to get rid of the bike. I didn't appreciate the way he did it, but watching my brother and most of my mates injure themselves regularly, I understood. I used to ride with them, but I never had the inkling to play a stunt-double myself. Soon after we got Ian home, Bob had finished his shift, and he stormed into the wood after us, a hammer in his hand. It didn't take very long. Ian must have been still waiting for the casts to go on, but even if he had been around to see it there was nothing he could have done about it. When he found out what had happened, the disappointment showed in his tearful eyes.

He didn't fare much better with bushes either. We used to go scrumping. We would eat apples and blackberries until we were full to burst, and then we would collect some more to take home. While we were picking apples, we noticed a shed behind the blackberry bush. So we decided to investigate. It was at the back of a run-down bungalow, and it was open. The whole place looked as if it had been abandoned decades ago. We found newspapers from the war. I found a couple of gin traps, as well as what looked like a collection of metal detecting finds, so I took them with me, and I went back to the apple tree, to chew on an apple while I pondered what I'd found. One by one the others would climb over or push their way through the bush.

Then, without warning, I was startled by an inhuman piercing scream. It turned out to be Ian, running through the bush. We had no idea what had happened. My first worry was that someone was chasing him. I knew I could probably outrun anyone on the other side, but even so, it wasn't a nice feeling. But Ian ran in a straight line and didn't stop until he collided with a tree. It wasn't until we picked him up off the ground, still screaming, that we realised his eyes were shut tight. On closer inspection, we saw that his hair was wet and sticky, and he smelled of creosote. We dragged him to a puddle, and helped him rinse his eyes. He must have knocked something hard enough for the creosote to go all over him. At the time I was in a panic; I thought he might never get to see again. Yet later on, I can picture his face appearing among the blackberries in the bush, and I would have to stifle a giggle. When we got home, he rinsed his eyes again, but because they were still stinging, he made the effort to calm down a little and then set off to the doctor to get his eyes cleaned properly. It took him a while to get over that, and in fact he behaved himself right up to the end of the week.

Whether we were all stupid or just daring, I wouldn't like to say, but it was a rare occasion if we all returned home without a mark or blemish of some sort. Colin was dared to climb a tree, in order to get some eggs out of a nest. He climbed up, found the nest, and then shouted down that she, the bird that is, hadn't laid any eggs. The slow, meticulous climb, and all that effort for nothing. We heard it before we saw anything. The noise seemed loud even though it was so far above us, but we all heard the branch under Colin start to crack. As if in slow motion, he fell on to the next one underneath, which then cracked, broke away, and he landed on the next, and so on, until the very last one. He landed on that one with a heavy thud. With legs hanging limp on either side, almost touching the ground, Colin opened his mouth and let out the tiniest 'ugh!' I, along with everyone else, was in agony with laughter. I know it was mean. He was really hurt, but watching him slide down the branches of that tree had me doubled up. Like most of the things we would end up doing, it was like watching a cartoon in real life.

Some days I was sure we would end up working for Acme manufacturers as seen in all the cartoons. Like the time I fell off the roof of a house, and I just stood up, and climbed the ladder again. I must have landed on the full length of my body, but it was only later that I realised I was bruised all over. I can remember the thud more than the fall. Derby just looked at me and said, 'no brain, and no feeling'. I didn't want to tell him that was just a coping mechanism. If I didn't use my brain, I wouldn't have to think, and therefore I wouldn't have to consider my feelings. Life was so much easier without them.

Even when we were older, we used to get up to all sorts, not necessarily to get into trouble, or to cause it, but sometimes it just happened that way. Just after I lost my job at the window manufacturing company, we all decided to go away for the weekend. We needed cheering up. We drove down to Margate, and we all sat in the back of the van, just having a chat, passing the time until we could think of something we'd like to do. Two police constables showed up, and told us that, basically, we were a nuisance. We were arrested for disturbing the peace, even though there was no-one else around, and I thought we were being quiet. The matter wasn't going to go any further, as long as we left Margate and didn't return to Kent.

I know I didn't have a normal childhood, and I suppose I took every chance to make up for lost time. In time I learnt to control myself enough to savour my freedom. Then there were times when I just got carried away with the rest of the gang. I must have been about eighteen when we decided to have a day out. By the end of the evening, we thought we might need feeding, so there was a unanimous vote for pizza. No-one can now remember how it started, but before long, we were in the middle of a food fight, hot sticky slices of pizza flying left and right.

But sometimes the boys had good intentions. On my return from a weekend away, I opened the door to the flat I was living in, to find it was full of beer. Barrels and bottles, even cans. The bath was full of beer. It may not have been the best way to get over something, but the boys meant well, and we went through every emotion that night. We even found Derby having a bath in the beer. If I remember rightly, someone may have mentioned, whilst sober, that beer is good for the skin and hair. Knowing Derby though, he wouldn't need a reason to bathe in beer.

Waking up in a pet shop warrants an explanation; yet I don't have one; at least, not a sensible one. It started off as a prank. It was supposed to be a practical joke. Apart from a slight shrug of the shoulder, that was the only thing they would tell me. They had sneaked into the flat, and left what seemed like, and smelled like, hundreds of animals.

I treasured being with the people I felt comfortable with. It was rare but precious. Yet I still wasn't happy to be around anyone. I had so much to learn about human interaction and communication. Long ago I gave up trying to make myself understood. I tried to relax enough just to be able to go along with what everyone else was doing. I hoped the disabling flashbacks would go unnoticed. I was grateful that for the most part they would ignore me until I was ready to join them again. They never asked what was happening, and I'm sure they put it down to some sort of quirk in my personality.

Something else that helped me cope a little easier was the range of activities that a probation officer had organised. His name was Doug, but unfortunately I have forgotten his surname. He used to take us shooting; we would get great target practice at the local range. Doug also set us projects to complete while we were with him. He taught us so much, but what I remember most of all, was that he gave us the benefit of doubt, and treated us all as individuals. He actually listened to what we had to say. He was not a soft touch - there was no way you could pull the wool over his eyes - but I was made to feel my thoughts were valid, and that I was respected as a person. This was something I felt I would never get from Bob and, because of Bob, Brenda wouldn't offer either.

Doug bought a dilapidated house in Wales, and took us all along to help him out. He kept us occupied while we were there and we worked hard because he deserved that much from us. This meant we didn't get into trouble while we were there, and we were learning without trying. I had a wonderful time. I felt I was an important part of the team, and, in turn, I learnt a little more about how to be around others.

My life had been, at least thus far, one stress after another. All the solutions I had come up with to get me through the day a little easier were temporary, or ineffective. I thought metal detecting might prove another diversion, so I was willing to give it a try. I found out about metal detecting quite by accident. I had been jittery. I knew I would have to start doing something or I would spend the rest of the day trying to escape my own thoughts. I was skimming through a book, just hoping and praying I would find something to distract me, and there it was - a short but simple description about the history that can be found with a metal detector. Everyone has a passion in their life, and even though it took me a while to work out what mine would be, as soon as I started I knew it would be a lifelong affair.

I knew the father of one of my friends had used a metal detector, but I didn't feel I could ask him about it. However curious, I would have to make my own way to the information. In any case, I found it easier to absorb information when I could work with it at my own pace. Instead, I read a little more, and when I saw a Viking metal detector in a second-hand shop, I didn't think twice about it. It cost me seven pounds, I think, but I wasn't concerned about the price. I felt I had read more than enough to know that I wanted to try it out. I just couldn't wait to start using it. On my way back from the shop, I was trying to imagine the sorts of things I would find. I tried to picture the world around me as it was long ago. I imagined finding goblets used by kings. I imagined what it would be like holding something that hadn't been held for hundreds of years. I would have been impressed with something that had been lost for decades, never mind centuries.

On my first venture with the Viking, I found three hammered coins, and I was hooked. It wasn't that I thought I had found a national treasure, it was the fact that it gave me the chance to have direct contact with history, and that was what I loved most of all.

At first I had no idea about placing the items I had found in a timeframe. I would have to ask around, and I started spending almost as much time in the library as I did with the Viking. I used to go to the museum regularly, to compare, and I felt so proud of myself when I knew that I had something similar to the exhibition in my own bedroom.

My year away meant I had to stop detecting, but once I was out again, it was as if I had never been away. It is difficult to explain why this is such a passion for me. I know there are people who would never even consider such a hobby, yet for me, I think I like the fact that I know I must be calm and I need to concentrate while searching, and at the same time I am actually trying to control my enthusiasm and excitement at the idea of what I may find. The idea that I may be the first to discover something vital in helping the rest of society understand our past a little better gives me the energy and willpower to fight anything else my mind may be trying to put me through. It is such a weird sensation, holding something in your hand and knowing you are the first person in centuries to have direct contact with it.

It is difficult to find out about a previous owner; very few items have identifying marks of ownership. There was one brooch I managed to trace to a French woman. She came to England and lived here for a while, which must have been when she lost the brooch.

So far, I have found all sorts of things, from most eras in our history. If I were pushed to choose, I would have to say that Roman finds were my favourite. I think what I admire most about them is that they were an organised power. Even two thousand years after their arrival we can see their influence in our own lives as well as evidence of their lives here. Something that proved unusual was an Egyptian ring. I can only imagine how it came to be in the Midlands. The Victorians were great enthusiasts of antiquity and recorded everything they imported back into the country, but as this ring was not listed, its journey to the place where I found it can only be imagined. From its shape and detailed carvings, it would seem to be a ceremonial ring, probably religious. It is of course quite likely that it came with the Romans, as they were known to both the Egyptians and us.

There was one beautiful pendant, still wearable and saleable. Within twenty minutes or so, I heard the familiar excited noise of the detector. I bent down, and soon I had a beautiful pendant in my hand. On our way home, someone stopped me to see what sort of luck I'd had. I showed him my find, and as soon as he got his breath back, he offered me four thousand pounds. I was astounded. Although tempting, I thought I should try to find out more about it. I had hoped it was unusual enough that it would have been recorded at some point in history; and that perhaps I could even find the name of an owner.

I have become a regular at the museum, as that is the first place I think of when I need information, although many times that proved not to be the case, especially if it was anything unusual, or even worse, fragmented. After searching for hours on end, and getting everyone involved who may be able to help, we found it to be medieval. In the end, some experts priced it at an incredible £72,000 pounds. Before it could all sink in, I found out it had been declared treasure trove, and now has pride of place in an exhibit in Coventry museum. The story was in the newspaper, and the photograph looked as if the passport office had approved it.

I just couldn't contain my excitement. I had found something that was pleasing to the eye and the pocket, and it will be safe in an exhibition for the following generations. I think the closest description of that feeling, when I walk past the case and see an artefact I have found, is a mixture of pride and awe. It is also a somewhat humble feeling. It is easy to see how we humans do not last very long, but we affect the world and our society for a long time after. I think history inspires me to find out more, and do more.

I was given the chance to visit an archaeological site in South Wales when I was younger. It was just as I had imagined it to be. The area was roped off, people all over the place kneeling on the ground, carefully searching for the tiniest fragments that would provide evidence of a previous life. Not too far away, others sat behind a long table, adding each find to the catalogue, giving it a reference number and then putting it away for safe keeping. The site was next to a church, and it was deemed an important search because planning permission was agreed in principle for another building to be erected. If the foundations had been laid, the site would have been lost for ever. I only spent the weekend with them, but what really surprised me was how everyone was so excited, yet no-one was frantic. There was no rushing around, no screaming and shouting, everyone looked calm on the surface. It was only when you looked into their eyes that you could see the excitement.

What I liked about that visit was the fact that I had been given the opportunity to meet with people who had the same passions as me, and knowing they were academics made me value my hobby even more. It proved to me that even if no-one at home was willing to support me, I knew I was doing something that others had chosen as a profession. I guessed if I kept it as a hobby, I wouldn't get caught in a rut and start to hate my job.

I have also been lucky enough to be the first to scan a site. I was detecting with some friends near Trycross Zoo. I would have been happy with just a coin or two, and as long as I didn't find anything that had been dropped the previous night, I would have been satisfied. After a while, for some unfathomable reason, I changed direction and there it was - a hoard of coins. I should have realised it was going to be special; there were lots of pottery fragments just on the surface. These things take a long time to organise, but to me at least, it seemed just days after I found the coins, the professionals were there, excavating a full site. Although sad that I personally couldn't go back on it, I was glad that I had found the remains of an historical site. I was eager to find out what they had come across, and they were kind enough to let me read the reports at a later stage. It turned out to be a Roman farmstead. They found remains of a house, and what they believed to be stables, and there was so much that showed what everyday Roman life in the Midlands was like. The original hoard, which was buried in the third or fourth century, was declared a national treasure, and therefore automatically belongs to the realm.

History, or evidence of it, is very much like an onion in its layers. On any one site, it is theoretically possible to find something from any and every period of our history. I find it easier to associate the items with a particular era, and then the era with dates.

Something that to me is a bit like the chicken and egg question, is the number of fertility symbols and charms I have found. It means that, either they worked and everyone had them, or they were no good and people threw them away. Luckily my frequent insomnia gives me the chance to ponder this question on a regular basis. Whichever it is, they crop up often. And just to prove this isn't just a historical thing, on one outing I found an aluminium vibrator, about two inches long – with batteries. So obviously not an historic piece, but it went in the same box as the rest.

I once found a Saxon ring, made from silver, which had been engraved with the letters L, A, A, and G. I assumed it was a form of identification, and have yet to be proved wrong. The letters seem to be a mystery. On another occasion, I found sixteen silver coins from the time of Henry the VIII. There was a pretty little gold pendant that springs to mind from a different outing, because it is not often that I find something like that, and for it to be whole and reasonably undamaged. I have been told it was worn as a good luck charm, and was the sort of thing that would have been buried with its owner. Mostly it was the likes of knights who had them, so they would wear the pendant into battle. That would explain why I didn't find the owner next to it. Other pendants similar to this one have been known to contain a lock of hair from a saint, or even holy water blessed to protect the wearer. It was common for the holy water to have been brought from Jerusalem by pilgrims.

I also found a gold coin under glass, this turned out to be a part of a bracelet, which would have been worn by Romans as a good luck charm. It is small and difficult to see, but in the right light, the gold glints just enough for it to get noticed.

It is quite easy to recognise the site of a battle. On it you are most likely to find a variety of items, from buckles and buttons, to brooches with holes in them. Individual coins, as well as small hoards, which would have been buried at the edge of the field, to collect later if the person were to survive. I use the word person, because throughout British history there have been women going into battle alongside their men folk. It was common for the warriors to hide all that they had so theft and pillaging would not occur.

Something that I found out about myself while metal detecting is that I can recognise different metals by texture, but I am completely insensitive to heat. Perhaps having to control my reaction to pain and other adverse sensations, I have subconsciously trained myself to ignore physical pain, and pain caused by heat especially. Even in the dark, I can tell immediately if I have found a hammered coin.

I had found something that meant I could be on the road to recovery. All I needed to do now was learn to act, react, and interact with other people - a long and difficult journey that would be worth the effort by the end.

Chapter Nine

Young Love

LIKE most boys of my age, I was capable of ignoring and dismissing girls the way I would an annoying fly. Then one day, like a bolt of lightning hitting me between the eyes, I noticed girls existed. I knew long before puberty had kicked in that there was a female to our species, but they were all related to me, or were already collecting their pensions. But after I became aware of them, they were everywhere. I couldn't turn in any direction without seeing one.

I hardly noticed puberty; most kids were bemoaning spots and having to fight the emotional overflow that I had curbed years before. Maybe I had the spots and the unrequited love, and the pining for a pop star like a puppy; I just don't remember. Others were complaining that no-one could or wanted to try to understand them. I could have told them there was no point in trying to make themselves understood, because no-one was interested, but I couldn't be bothered. I had reached a state of apathy. It was almost as if I had realised the world was ignoring me, and as I wasn't a part of it, it didn't matter.

Now and again, the odd feeling broke through the barriers, but like the little Dutch boy with his finger in the dam, I was more or less on top of it. I guess what I'm trying to say is that by the time I got to sixteen, I wasn't as overwhelmed by my emotions and feelings as I had been. They were no less intense, but I just got better at hiding them.

I didn't realise I could be attractive or interesting to girls, but, as it turned out, I never had to do any chasing. Although never comfortable with intimacy and trust, I was grateful that this generation of girls was emancipated and not afraid to ask.

My first love was a girl called Lisa. Unfortunately for me, we only got together about a month before I went inside. I didn't think it would go anywhere, but she was still around when I came out, so we started where we left off. The relationship was not just intimate, and it could have been almost stifling. We spent all our time together.

We met through Mark the builder. I was helping him with some work he was doing on his own house. It was a sunny day, and the work was enjoyable. Two girls appeared and hovered for a while, just watching. Mark kept asking them if either had a boyfriend, and they would giggle and mumble something, still keeping their distance. I'd noticed them too, well, one especially - Lisa as it turned out to be. Mark had his eye on the other girl, but for him it wasn't meant to be. Because teenagers can't or won't have any direct social interaction with someone they like until they're sure the feeling is mutual, Lisa set off something along the lines of Chinese Whispers in order for me to do something about it.

Lisa told her friend Debbie, and Debbie told Mark; Mark then went into a bit of a 'nudge nudge, wink wink, say no more' type of routine, until I got the message. Once the awkward introduction was over, we just sort of ended up together. It was nice of course to have found someone who liked me. I spent a lot of time with a new crowd. Lisa's brother Jeff, and Mark, would organise model car races, which meant they put the Scalextric set to very good use. It was up in the attic and, now and again, they would take it apart to put back together as a different race track.

They would ask me to help them out, and this made me feel more accepted within the group. I felt welcome there, and this in turn helped me become better acquainted with normal social interaction. I found it difficult, having spent so much time by myself, and I sometimes felt I would struggle to hold a conversation properly. After years of acting and reacting to what was going on inside my head, I lacked the confidence I needed to mix with others. I was so used to Bob barking at me, and Brenda dismissively mumbling something or other, that when it came to real people, I worried.

When you spend the time after the complete destruction of your childhood, just waiting to become an adult while avoiding getting beaten, and avoiding physical intimacy because you fear it, your sense of reality is warped and distorted. Before talking to anyone I would have to ignore my own viewpoint, and think what sort of answer would be acceptable. I suppose I realised quite early on that what had become normal for me, didn't necessarily happen to other people. I knew I wasn't in any way unique, but even so, what I had been through was not everyday subject matter for light conversation.

I got on well with Lisa and her family, and in fact they let me move into their home. Lisa's father got me a road-sweeping job with the council. It obviously wasn't my first choice of career, but it paid a wage and I could cope with the workload, although I really didn't see myself in that job until retirement.

Without me even realising it, things had become more serious. I had no problem with that; after all, it wasn't forced on me, and I was happy to go along with it. We set up our own home; the changes to the relationship were seamless, with one incident blended into another, and I was grateful I didn't have to do anything about it.

During this time, I got friendly with a lad from Bedworth, and Lisa made it clear that she didn't like that sort of company. I know that, after my spell inside, the last thing we wanted was for me to get caught doing something I shouldn't have been, but I wasn't willing to give up my new friendship, whatever the consequences. I guess Lisa had my best interests in mind, but she also understood that I needed my space away from her. She waited patiently for me to realise myself that I had things I needed to get out of my system.

I was living in an age and personal environment that exuded aggression and violence. By the time I got to puberty, punk was all the rage and it suited me more than anything else. I took a particular liking to the Sex Pistols, and I liked the costume that style of music provided. I was comfortable in drainpipes and tee shirts that showed the world I couldn't care less about anything. I started to fall out with lots of people, mostly because I was sick of having to justify the way I was. Most people judge others on first impressions, and if they didn't like what they saw, they lost interest in the person, and just obsessed about the image.

I found the perfect outlet for my frustration at still not being accepted or acceptable. Fighting - that was the answer. Punching someone in the face is so therapeutic. At least that was what Bob had taught me. I had an excess of anger and aggression, and as there seemed to be so many others in the same situation, I was never short of opponents.

On one occasion we drifted along to the service station, and there was an altercation between us, that is, the usual crowd, and some Asians. They were already men, and we were in that awkward stage where we were no longer boys, but not yet men. They were saying something, loud enough for us to hear, and their gestures alone were enough to set our hackles up. Yet we couldn't be sure we could understand them. Derby and I stopped to fight, the others blended into the background. There was all the usual sizing up; most of what went on was an exchange of nasty facial expressions that set the mood before it gets physical if neither backs down.

It sort of fizzled out, and then someone on the sidelines stepped in to officially declare an end to the fight. We left to go home, and nearby there was a roadworks site. Derby pinched a pickaxe, and walked casually away. I don't think anyone noticed. We met up with Ian and Wally again, and all started toward home.

The Asians were a little way ahead of us, and they were on pushbikes. We were still outraged at their provocation, and we refused to drop it. So we thought we should cut them up on a steep road. Two of their bikes ended up getting intimate with a lamppost; one laid his bike by the road, and the biggest stayed on his bike, shouting he was going to kill us. Perhaps seeing we were kids, he thought he would scare us. I had been hearing the same thing for years, and it meant nothing to me. I rolled my eyes – big deal – so someone else wants to kill me. I walked up to him and his bike, and I threw a punch that knocked him clear of the bike, and straight into a ditch. The others ran off, leaving the one in the ditch to come to by himself. We saw no movement for what seemed like a long time, and then, very slowly, a green turban rose out of the ditch. Derby took a swing at the turban with a pickaxe, but he missed, thank God.

I was starting to feel really guilty about what I had done, so I went over to the man in the ditch and I helped him out. We got talking because I wanted to know what he had against us when he didn't even know us. We bought a couple of rounds of drinks, well, that is they went in to get the drinks, as we were known to be underage, and we sat in the car park and talked. We found out they were living nearby, and we would be heading in the same direction to get home. It seems that ever since they arrived, they have been shunned and discriminated against because they were different. It rang so true. I could sympathise when they told me people assumed they were stupid if they couldn't make themselves understood. I was beginning to see that, when I got home I could remove the clothes and the attitude, but they couldn't leave their skin.

There was only one problem with this realisation, but I wasn't willing to do anything about it because I was still nursing my own painful wounds. We were able to become friends though, and even the age difference wasn't much of an obstacle. Apart from Lisa, there was no-one I could feel close to. I felt as if I had no family, and for a while I was comfortable with that notion; if mine was a typical family, I didn't need it.

Ian by this time had moved as well, and when I did see him he seemed different. It was something elusive; I couldn't put my finger on it, but there was something not quite right. When he finally received the diagnosis, he told me he had cancer. The doctors had told him he was suffering from a cancer of the glands, and that it is usually brought about by some sort of knock. I wanted to laugh. A knock! That just proved to be typical English understatement. Approximately ten years of daily beatings, and the doctors say this illness is brought about by a knock.

Luckily, he took well to the treatment, and although harrowing, he made it through. Bob was nowhere in sight, and Brenda was at the Bingo Hall, hoping she could win enough to keep herself supplied with drink and fags until her next outing. Ian never told me how that made him feel, but to me it was just like water off a duck's back.

Lisa and I shared the same space, but it could be said we lived separate lives. She worked long hours as a hairdresser, and by the time she got home, she wouldn't be in the mood for socialising. I wasn't any better. I found it easier to exhaust myself physically on a daily basis; that way I would be too tired to take any notice of my thoughts and memories.

We worked hard trying to set up the sort of home we wanted, and then someone broke in, and the destruction was devastating. They took everything, even the toilet paper. We decided to move to Coventry, in the hope that a clean break would mean we could get over it more easily. Apart from anything else, we had to save to make our new home somewhere we liked being. Burglary is a violation of space, and, as I found out to my horror, that feeling stays long after the actual incident, whether you stay in that space or not.

We would go out together once in a blue moon, and perhaps subconsciously I wanted to avoid the fate of my own parents and that of Brenda and Bob. I hoped if I didn't spend all my spare time drinking, I wouldn't turn out to be like either of them. It worried me often enough that my temper was at times just as extreme and vicious as Bob's. I tried to persuade myself that nature is stronger than nurture. If it had been a choice of turning out like my father or Bob, I prayed it would be the former.

I was becoming more comfortable mixing with others, as long as it was on a superficial level. I thought things were going well. I believed it was a stable relationship, and I was happy. Obviously Lisa wasn't. On my way home one day, I felt the urge to take a different route to my usual one. It was as if I was being pushed, shoved, and dragged in the other direction. Not a hundred yards in front of me, I found Lisa in another man's arms. Watching her kiss someone else made me feel like my insides were imploding. The vacuum created by the lack of trust I had in others, compounded with Lisa's betrayal, was an experience ugly like no other. I wanted to be strong; I wanted desperately to get past it, to carry on as if nothing had happened. My father had made the same effort with Brenda, but I hoped Lisa would be different. The next morning I went to work, hoping that when I got back, we could talk it over and try again. But by the time I got home, she had already moved her things out.

From that moment on, all I needed in my life was fast cars, fast booze, and fast women. I just wanted to rush through life doing as much as possible, without having to experience anything. I even got around to trying Hash. I was willing to try anything that would get rid of the heavy empty feeling inside, where my emotions used to be.

I had one bad experience with drugs, and to be honest there are moments when it still scares me, even now. I was offered a tea made from some sort of mushroom; my mate never told me exactly what it was, just that it would be a trip I would never forget. He made it sound like a good thing, so I agreed. He brought the mug over to me, and as I drank it, I thought it had a strange bitter taste. I wasn't interested in the taste. I thought of it the same way I would medicine; I was eager to see what the effects would be.

It didn't take long - the first thing I noticed was my feet getting jittery. I jumped up. I knew I had to move. I felt trapped; the walls were creeping in on me, the ceiling getting ready to drop and crush me. The air I was breathing felt like ribbons sliding down my throat. I was suffocating. I needed to get out. I wanted to escape. There was only one thing I could do, and that was run. I couldn't move fast enough, and everything was in my way. As I ran down the street, the houses on either side were leaning in, not leaving me enough room to breathe. Smells I wouldn't normally notice filled my nostrils, stretching the flesh as if it were solid. I could see nothing and everything all at the same time. Like my life, everything around me was blurred, yet also focused. The cacophony of sounds in my ears seeped in, filling every space in my head until I heard nothing. Each and every pore in my skin seemed to tear as the sweat poured out as if someone had opened a set of floodgates. I ran and ran and ran.

Water, I needed water. I was hot, I was thirsty, I was running with no idea where I wanted to go. I recognised a door, realising I knew how to use it, and that there may be water behind it. I pushed it, nothing. I slammed into it with my shoulder, and I got in. As if I knew my way around, I found a container and emptied it over my head. I was still running, so I was out before I was in, the cooling water evaporated as it hit my skin, giving only momentary relief. Back on the street, I continued running. My thoughts had cleared a little, and I knew why I was running. I needed to escape; everything around me was a threat to my life. There was nothing, nor anyone, I could trust, not even myself. Lights glared into my eyes, making them sting, and my mouth was dry, each breath scratching its way down.

At last my brain managed to retrieve the SOS message from my muscles, and I slowed down. A big mistake; once I stopped, all the muscles seized. I knew at that moment that whatever I was trying to escape from would destroy me. Then calm. A perfect calm.

The following morning was very much a morning after the night before. I was worse for wear. I think the running was worse than the actual tea. I got to thinking that, even though I had never experienced fear like I had the night before, the tea brought down the barriers that stopped me doing what I had wanted to do ever since Ison first touched me. Without the inhibitions that caged my mind, I did what anyone in my situation would have done. It took me a long time to realise that what I feared the most was actually my own memories and the flashbacks.

The memory of the last time Ison tried anything sprang to mind. I wanted to avoid him, I wanted to escape. It took an amazing amount of strength to move his hand from my thigh. He tried again, but this time all subtlety had gone out of the window. He placed his hand between my legs, cupping my genitals through my trousers. I stood up, looked him straight in the eyes, and told him no. I had managed to make it clear to Ison when he brought the puppy that what he did wasn't going to happen again. So I knew I was in no physical danger; I knew I no longer needed to fear him, or Bob for that matter. I could see that I hadn't spent the previous night running away from a person. Being under the influence of a drug made me see how desperately I wanted to get away from my own thoughts.

Chapter Ten

Hope

MY RELATIONSHIP with Lisa ended so abruptly that the last thing I wanted was to get involved again. I was happy just to spend a little time with someone; I made it clear I wasn't ready to commit and I was only interested in the short term. No-one had a problem with that. I suppose when you know what sort of relationship you want, you can tell the other person, and they can either accept or decline the offer.

So, for that little while, when I was doing the chasing, I was happy. And then I was caught off guard. A sucker for punishment, I went to visit Brenda and Bob, although by this time my relationship with them had disintegrated into simple and trivial banter. I stepped outside for some fresh air; it was hard to believe you could suffocate in such a shallow conversation.

I leaned against the rail surrounding the green, watching a young woman play football with a small child. I recognised her, but only from dim and distant memory. She was familiar because she lived in the same street as Brenda and Bob. Slowly, snippets of information came to me. Her brother was at school with me, the family was from some part of Yugoslavia, they were all more or less pleasant enough to talk to. By which point she must have noticed me, and came over to say hello.

Nada, which she explained to me, means hope in English, asked me if I wanted to kick a ball with her and her son Lee. I looked at the little kid, wide-eyed and enthusiastic to play, and, for his sake, I didn't want to refuse. It is easy to say with hindsight that some decisions are wrong from the very beginning. Had I known what would be waiting for me just around the corner, I would have turned and run in the other direction.

But if life was simple, we would all die of boredom.

Lee was a happy child, and like myself at his age, loved to whiz around, making everyone dizzy, just from watching him. I played football, for a while, and was getting ready to disappear when Nada said that they will be seeing me again, shortly. She was so emphatic that I didn't even consider ignoring her or refusing.

I was to find out soon that most Serbs are like that. The diction of their language is such that it is easy enough for an English ear to hear an opinion stated as fact. Nada may well have expected me to dispute everything and anything she may have said to me. But by the time I had learnt to recognise the Serbian rhythm in her English speech, it was probably too late.

It wasn't too long before we were living together. We got on well, and I liked being around Lee. I hoped I could at least be a good example to him. I was very aware of my every reaction and interaction with him. It was all I could do to stop myself from comparing my behaviour to Bob's. I was desperate to ensure I would learn from my experiences. I had missed out on my own childhood, and I wasn't willing to let anything ruin his, nor that of any other child I would have close contact with.

Her whole family was very welcoming, even if they were a little overwhelming with their hospitality. Nada is actually a child from a mixed marriage, a Serbian father and English mother. I found out that Nada's father, Milan, had fought in the Second World War, and he fascinated me with his stories of the front lines in the Balkans. He even showed me the scars he had earned while he was ambushing the enemy from inside the frequent wooded copses. The terrain in the Balkans, as he went on to explain, is ideal for close combat. Anyone who gets to know the lay of the land has a serious advantage. The Germans, or anyone else for that matter, wouldn't stand a chance without air power.

That was only one bone of contention between us. I have to admit I admired the Germans, and still do. I can read about Hitler and his armies in a book, and I can look at it objectively. Milan, on the other hand, hates them with a vengeance. I can understand this; he fought in a war against the Germans, and every day during that war he was aware of the fact that each could be his last. He taught me all about a Serbian type of spiteful stubbornness which they call *inat*. This is when you insist on something until the other person gives in, and then you refuse to accept their submission, because it took them so long to realise you were in the right. All in all, a complete waste of time because nothing moves on. Although, from some of the examples he gave from seeing it on the front lines, it seems it has even saved lives. This *inat* doesn't appear very often, but it is fascinating to watch, and I find it amusing to see it in non-Serbs. I think it must be a universal phenomenon, so it seems odd to me that we don't have our own word for it.

The history of the Balkans in general, and of the Serbs especially, shows they are a very passionate nation. They seem to find apathy and indifference difficult. They love and hate with the same intensity, and that is probably why every generation fights its own war. Nada was no different; her emotions dragged her kicking and screaming through life, and for a little while, I got caught up in the vortex.

No more than a week had gone by since that first football game, when a man turned up at my mother's door demanding to know what Nada was doing with me when she was still living with him. I didn't know what to think. I had only popped in for a chat with Brenda. This man was so sure of himself that even I thought he was believable. I asked Nada what she had to say about it, and she told me he was crazy because I should realise she was living with her parents when we met. Nada was so certain of what she was saying that I started doubting the man at my door. Her mother confirmed it all, so I persuaded myself it was just a mistake on his part, and I made myself pretend it had never happened.

After four months together we were engaged, and that was when I started noticing she had problems of her own. Two people, fighting their own demons, have no time or emotion to spare for a relationship involving another person. During one argument, she just blurted out how she never wanted to get engaged, and how she still loved the man she was involved with previously. Before I had a chance to react, I left. No more than two days had gone by when she was back again, begging me to take her back; she knew then she had made a mistake. Nada is capable of going from one extreme emotion to another at the speed of light. There were days when I struggled to keep up with her moods and emotions.

Like a moth to a light bulb, I took her back. When I told my mates, they all let out one low unanimous groan. Plans were made for the wedding, even though people had hinted to me that Nada wasn't the loyal or stable type. Just as I had remembered him being as a child, my brother Ian was a man of few words on any subject, but his opinion was concise and clear when it came to my relationship with Nada. It would come to no good; it will be a mistake. I had never asked him, and Ian was too polite to volunteer his own opinion, but I was sure he didn't like her. When I invited him to the wedding, he told me he wouldn't bother buying a present, because if I had any sense I would realise that even a bottle of wine would last longer than a marriage doomed as much as the one I was planning.

Derby especially made an enormous effort to stop me getting involved. He kept telling me not to marry her; he obviously knew more than I did. At the time, he was on a warrant for something or other, and as the police turned up at his door, he escaped through a window and ran all the way to my house to warn me one last time.

He lived in Bedworth, roughly five miles away. The police had caught him off guard, he was hoping to get to speak to me before disappearing, but instead he jumped out of an upstairs window in just his underpants. Just in case he didn't look silly enough running barefoot through the town, God made it rain all that day. So there he was, standing outside my house in soaking underpants, throwing pebbles at my window, in order to get my attention. At first I wasn't sure if I could hear anything or not, but I thought it best to check, just to make sure.

When I looked down, all I could see was Derby, shivering in his sodden boxers, telling me first of all not to go through with the marriage, and secondly, asking if I had some clothes he could borrow. I let him in; he was dripping rain on my carpet, and asking if I had a pair of boots I wouldn't miss for a while. It wasn't until I looked at him closely that I realised he had nothing on except his underpants. I gave him a pair of tracksuit bottoms and a pair of boots, the kind Puss in Boots wore, with the flap that folds over. It was only when I saw him three years later that I found out he had gone to Newcastle that same night.

I should have realised he was serious; after all he was putting his own liberty at risk to save my neck. I was just too stupid to see how much my neck needed saving. I waved him off, and then thought no more about it. Everyone was against it, down to the very last one. If I had heard just one positive comment, perhaps I would have been a little more objective about it. As it was, it was me against the world. I wanted to believe that a marriage would be the ideal opportunity to make a fresh start in my already damaged life. I hoped that Nada, too, was willing to make an effort as it was her second marriage.

Nada is a demonstrative woman, and it would take less than a blink of an eye for her to choose something to break, or aim at me. Her moods would swing wildly as if they were hanging from a bungee cord. It seemed to me that, since the moment we got married, I would have no idea what would be the right thing to do. I didn't understand why she was feeling the way she was; she was too involved with herself to even consider telling me. I had the impression I was supposed to know what I had done wrong. I would panic in case I had lost vital information for my present, during one of my still frequent flashbacks.

It took me a long time to recognise her triggers, but there were days when, certainly, I was glad I had grown up with Bob because at least he didn't have a monthly cycle. There was one incident I managed to block out of my memory, until a relative kindly brought it up again. I was at home when Nada rushed towards me with a snooker cue. I knew what was coming because I had seen it all before. I didn't even hear the blows land because of the ranting and raving. Her voice would be ringing in my ears, and the bruises would be thumping under the skin, finding their way to the surface.

I was terrified that Nada was right, and, as she had been telling me so often, that I was just imagining things to be worse than they were. It was all justified; she treated me only the way I deserved, at least that was the mangled message in amongst the barrage of verbal abuse. On a bad day, my mind would interchange her voice and face for Bob's. When it came down to it, there wasn't much of a difference between them. I can't remember having a good night's sleep very often, and it unnerved me when Nada would hit me while I was sleeping. It was difficult enough to deal with in the cold light of day, when I was awake and ready for it, but during my time with Nada there was many a night I was grateful to be suffering from insomnia. When she wasn't lashing out, which was rare, she would burst into tears, heaving racking sobs jerking her body until at last she would fall asleep.

There was another incident when I came through the front door to find Nada storming towards me with a large kitchen knife. Once again I had no idea what I had done wrong, but I guess I'd had plenty of practice living with Bob to recognise a danger sign and head for cover. I probably didn't, but thinking about it later it felt as if I ran in and out of every room, before escaping through an upstairs window. I was lucky enough to land on my feet.

I spent many nights on a sofa, usually Ian's, and I was uncomfortable because I knew that he knew, and even worse, his wife Kay knew. We never talked about it, but it was blatantly obvious. I didn't demean myself by telling them that I had walked into a door, or even slipped down the stairs. They would have looked down on me for lying so badly. It was easier to keep quiet.

On one such evening, as I sat on Ian's sofa trying to find a position where I wasn't pressing on this bruise or that, Kay asked me if I remembered the first time the two sisters-in-law had met. I had my fingers wrapped around a steaming mug of tea, and I listened to her explain how she saw my wife. As she went further into the story, I was remembering more and more about it. Ian and Kay had recently got together, and they came by to see us. Nada had been out, and Ian decided to go next door to speak to his friend. Kay excused herself and went to the bathroom. Before she came back, Nada came home. Even before stepping through the door, she was screaming at me at the top of her voice. Poor Kay was probably too scared to come out immediately, and when she did, Nada turned towards her and then back to me, and demanded to know what she was doing there. Kay was getting flustered but managed to tell her she was visiting with Ian.

I noticed after that visit, Nada started to make a big effort with Kay; she was trying to be friendly, but I'm sure Kay found her clingy and overbearing. There was even talk of going away on holiday together. Ian was insistent on keeping his distance, and I just wanted to keep the peace.

I thought when she became pregnant, things would get better; perhaps if she had something positive to focus on, she would give me some breathing space. I was just stupid to overlook the hormones. Pregnancy affects women in different ways, and I know it can't be easy to go through it, but to me it felt like nine years rather than nine months. It seemed to be an agonising punishment, and I just couldn't remember why I was being punished. I can honestly say that up to that point in my life, finding out Nada was pregnant was the best thing that had happened to me. I was willing to go through hell on earth because nothing would mean more to me than my own child. There was one thought, and one thought only, that kept me sane and passive during that time. It was knowing that the two of us had produced a life; we put two tiny cells together and they were growing into a brand new person. There was nothing that was going to get in the way of me being a part of this child's life. Not even the other parent.

Nada gave birth to a son, and we named him Justin. I was with her during the labour and birth. Since then I have to say I admire women in a slightly different way. I don't know how I made it through that birth, and I was only watching!

As soon as he was born, they wrapped him up, handed him to me, and more or less shoved me out of the room. Nada had haemorrhaged, and she was losing blood faster than they could pour it in. In total she lost about eight pints. I know it was more important for them to save her life than explain to me what was going on, but those minutes of not knowing were probably some of the scariest in my life.

I only found out much later that she went into shock, which lead to post-natal depression. Nada was given medication for it, but I can't be sure if she took it regularly, if at all. Coping with depression can't be easy, especially after something like giving birth. Nada was, and is again, a strong and wilful woman, but when I thought I was being considerate in offering to help, I realise now that perhaps all I did was to emphasise her fears of not being able to cope. If I kept quiet it was the wrong thing, because I wasn't interested in her. When I asked her anything, I was interfering and criticising. It didn't take me very long to realise I could do nothing right. I felt unappreciated, unwanted, and I was no more than a chore-like imposition in her life.

Looking back, I can't imagine how I ever thought I could manage living with her moods and feelings when Nada herself couldn't. Things went from bad to worse, to almost impossible. We moved back to Keresley, so she could be close to her mother. In fact she had always had a very close relationship with Sadie, and it would often remind me of Lucy and Brenda. I was willing to do anything to get the relationship stable, if not for me, then because the boys deserved to grow up in a peaceful environment.

If at any time I mentioned that things were not quite right, she would say it was me, or my imagination. Her best form of defence was attack. She would tell me I was to blame, and that I was making her the way she was. As glass and crockery shattered against the walls, it was a real struggle not to believe her. I felt I was going to go mad. It was hard work persuading myself it might not be my fault. Though to be fair, when I tried to make contact with Justin about a decade later, Nada actually took the time to explain to me that she had been ill, and had suffered a long time, including having to endure a stay in an institution.

I hoped that going abroad on holiday would help things along, because at the time it never crossed my mind that Nada's behaviour was due to an illness. Rather I was beginning to think it was just my bad luck to marry a female version of Bob, with TNT between her ears.

We took the boys with us; after all Justin was still a couple of months away from his first birthday. I tried to imagine how I would have felt if my parents had left me behind to go on holiday, and I didn't have the heart to leave them. Whilst on holiday, we took a day trip to a shrine dedicated to a saint. It was in a low dark cave on the island of Fuerte Ventura. The entrance to the cave was behind a church which had been added later. A tour guide explained that the cold cave was the perfect environment for the sarcophagus. There was a huge difference in the temperatures inside and out. I only got as far as catching sight of the body under glass, when someone pointed out to me that I had a blister on my leg.

I stepped away from the crowd, and I realised I was covered from head to foot in blisters. The largest of them covered most of my thigh. Apart from these blisters, I had no other symptoms and felt nothing out of the ordinary. Even though I was disgusted by the sight of them, I couldn't help being fascinated by the fact that some of the blisters were up to an inch high. They had filled with fluid, and were soft and malleable. By this time, others had begun to make a fuss, and the holiday rep called a doctor. Through an interpreter I was told it was because of the temperature difference, but people all around me were whispering it had something to do with the saint. I tried telling them I didn't believe, but people kept saying it was some sort of sign. Some were avoiding me, whilst others tried to get much closer. I was uncomfortable with the attention, especially when the next morning my body was as if nothing had happened. I had a dull headache which I assumed was due to dehydration. There was so much fluid under a very thin layer of skin, but there was no sign of any damage.

I thought about it; perhaps the doctor was right and the blisters were a natural phenomenon caused by the temperature. But then I thought back to all those times I had struggled to stay inside a church without passing out. If it hadn't been for Nada and her family I don't think I would have spent more than ten minutes in a church. Milan and Nada are lucky in that they believe. For a believer it is all simple, but for someone like me there are always questions that need answers, or even worse, better answers than I have already received.

I feel uncomfortable inside a church, and I think I put that down to the fact that, as a child, a church was something to walk past unless we had been invited to a wedding, a funeral, or a christening. Yet the Serbian Orthodox church in Birmingham struck me as impressive. Decorated from floor to ceiling in icons, with each one surrounded by a golden frame, and the sombre subjects painted in the brightest of colours. There is no seating, the whole congregation stands throughout the service. What also surprised me were the trays of burning candles to the side. Nada explained to me later that each lit candle represented a prayer of peace for the souls already departed, or for the good health of those still living. The whole building had a calming atmosphere.

I needed calming down by this point in my relationship with Nada. It was becoming obvious that the whole of the county knew she was cheating on me. Whenever I asked her, she would tell me to trust her, that there was nothing ever going on. More and more often she would go out by herself, and every time she was dressed to the nines.

On one such night, she was in such a rush to get away that she didn't even bother getting the boys settled. This made me angry; they had both been vomiting and suffering from diarrhoea the whole day and I knew they wanted to be comforted by their mother.

Nada had dismissed me as much as the boys, more or less telling me that if she wanted to go out clubbing, there was nothing I could do about it. Nada always took special care regarding her appearance. She was meticulous about detail, and her short thick hair and nails were always immaculate. Her dark hair and colouring meant she could easily wear even the brightest of trends. When it came to clothes, money was no object. It didn't even matter that there was no money for the mortgage; Nada had an image to uphold. She slammed the door shut on her way out. I waited until the boys were asleep, and I phoned Brenda to ask if she could be in the house just in case either of them woke up. Brenda told me she couldn't, so I asked her if I could borrow her car. I made sure the boys were sound asleep, found a neighbour who was willing to wait with the boys until I got back, and then drove into town.

I had no idea where I was going. It was as if something was guiding me. I knew instinctively which roads to turn into. And there she was. In a parked car, talking to some bloke, her top wrapped around her neck. All I could think was, that's where my hands should be. I wouldn't know where to begin in trying to justify what I did next. It was a stupid, spontaneous, and surreal reaction. I rammed his car. I have no idea what I wanted to achieve with that, but it felt good when I heard that heavy metallic thump as my car shuddered to a halt, and I jerked against the steering wheel and slumped back into the seat. I got out and walked away, without looking at what I had done.

I could imagine their two faces, frozen with shock, open-mouthed and staring, first at each other, then at my mother's car, jammed against both doors on the driver's side. The next morning, she turned up at the door and said she wanted to take the boys to sit with Sadie. All she had to say to me was that I shouldn't have interfered, and I owed the man a new car.

I started to wonder if maybe I should have the word 'mug' tattooed on my forehead, because surely there were people on this planet who couldn't quite make it out. At times like this I was sure fate had already decided no torture was too good for me. It would have been so easy for me to fall back on self-pity, and give up on my life. But if Nada had made it clear she didn't want me to be a part of her life, I was certain I was going to be in Justin's.

Chapter Eleven

A New Start

AS NADA and I waited for my first child to be born, I tried to take notice of what was going on in the world. If he or she would ever ask me, I wanted to be able to tell him, or her, what had happened. So in October of 1988, Boy George was at the top of the charts. Prince Charles slammed the latest trends in London's architecture, and the Turin shroud was declared a fake. It was believed to be a medieval creation of anywhere between 1260 and 1390. Some even believed it to be one of Da Vinci's practical jokes.

Peter Wright was fighting against a book ban for his memoirs; obviously there were MPs who thought his frank and matter-of-fact style would make some of them look like fools. The House of Lords took his side though and voted against the ban of *Spycatcher*. General Pinochet was finally usurped, so Chile would soon change, but back home, Margaret Thatcher was still in power, as was Ronald Reagan. In the Soviet Union, Mikhail Gorbachev was elected president, and the pop group, Bros, ruled the hearts of all teenage girls in the UK.

Like any year, 1988 had its ups and downs. An Egyptian became the first Arab novelist to win a Nobel Prize for literature, and Salman Rushdie published his *Satanic Verses*, which led to a fatwah being declared. Global warming was recognised, and named for the first time, but we wouldn't need to worry about it, because doctors were able to start prescribing Prozac. Before long it was to become the new antibiotic, much like grey had become the new black.

The evening news was made more interesting by the incident of Sue Lawley being attacked by lesbian protesters, and, on a sad note, it seemed that just as the Iran – Iraq war was ending, another was about to begin.

There were ethnic clashes in Karachi, and even closer to home the parliament in Belgrade was besieged by angry workers demanding the resignation of government. In Prague, the riot police had to use tear gas to control the demonstrators, and throughout the world everyone hoped Europe wouldn't escalate into war.

I also took more of an interest in the history and culture of the Serbs, as well as the English; I wanted to understand the cultures my child would be a part of. I didn't want to answer any question with 'I'm not sure'. I have to admit, it was the Serbian cuisine I adapted to very easily. Much like their emotions, the Serbs also enjoy food at both ends of the spectrum. There seems to be nothing delicate on their menu. Food is either hot, as in spicy, or sour or salty, or very sweet. The other thing about it is the huge portions. There is nothing better for a Serbian host than for a guest to accept an offer of another portion. What also helps is their concept of food being something to be savoured. Taste is something to relish and remember. Food is a communal pastime. I was uncomfortable with this, but mealtimes, having something to do whilst in the company of others, made it easier to be around people.

None of this was all that important now that I held my son in my arms. I stood on the other side of the door while they tried to save Nada's life in the very room she had given life to my son. The amount of blood that had soaked through the bed and flowed to the floor was frightening. The most awful thing about it was, as I turned back just one last time to see her before they shut the door, all I could sense was the blood pouring out faster and faster.

I was surrounded by chaos which is most likely an everyday occurrence in a hospital. People were rushing around, and there was so much noise and commotion. I can't be sure if it happened quickly or slowly; it was all over in an instant, and yet seemed to drag on for hours all at the same time. It was the sort of memory, however your mind played it back to you, that remained clear and in focus.

Yet holding Justin in my arms, I was calm. Deep inside, I was worried about Nada; I realised what had happened wasn't in any way normal because of the number of people that went into the room once I had left it. There was no-one around for me to ask what was going on, so I was left to imagine the worst and hope for the best.

The overwhelming feeling I had at that moment was so powerful and so striking, that even now, over fifteen years later, remembering it stops the breath in my throat. It is the realisation that you are holding a brand new person in your arms, and that this little person depends on you for food, water, warmth, and comfort. It truly needs nothing else, but that is the moment when you realise, whatever they ask of you, you will provide.

I realised I didn't know this tiny person lying in my arms just yet, but I was grateful that I had the rest of my life to get to know him. Justin opened his eyes, and to me it seemed as if he looked straight into mine. I knew my life had changed forever, and couldn't imagine that things wouldn't just get better and better.

He was no more than the length of my forearm, and I was scared to hold him. It was just as frightening to change him. That first nappy was like something out of a Hammer Horror film. Hitchcock would have been proud. I was frightened at the thought of having to feed him, but at the same time I was excited at the prospect of being a father. He was so tiny; he seemed fragile and delicate. Yet when I think back, it seems that even by the hour, he was growing stronger. I was happy just to sit and look at him lying in my arms. I could watch him sleep, my eyes following the relaxed but regular rise and fall of the tiny ribcage, and I noticed my own breathing would change to the rhythm of the baby.

This was a major change for me; before Justin was born, I avoided sitting at all. I didn't want to relax because that would have meant my thoughts would wander, and the last thing I wanted was to have to fight my way out of a flashback. It worried me that I would let my son down, by getting caught up in my fears, rooted to the spot by my own horrific memories.

Even if Nada had been well, I would have been involved with the night time feeds and the nappy changes. After all I had had nearly nine months to get used to the idea that another person would be joining the family. I hoped Lee would be oblivious to any changes in my behaviour towards him. He didn't deserve to be treated any differently just because I had a child of my own, so I made a special effort with him.

I could remember all too well what I had gone through with Bob so I didn't want to put anyone through that, especially not a small child. Maybe I was overprotective of both the boys, but my own childhood experiences seemed still fresh and raw in my mind. Day or night, my mind would disappear into itself, as if it was playing the same tape over and over again, except it could never be wiped clean. It was as if I needed to keep them safe for my own sake as well as theirs. I wanted to prove to myself that I would be able to put all those bad experiences to good use.

There were days when I doubted I would be a good father. There were days when I wondered if I deserved to be a father at all. After all, I'd had no role model to speak of. Once my mother had moved us away, my own father broke off all contact and I always felt he gave up too easily. On the other hand, Bob's idea of interaction with a child was 'if with fist you don't succeed, hit, hit, and hit again'. There was only one thing I felt worthy enough to be counted as a positive lesson from Bob, and that was how he managed not to treat us any differently from his own child. I would have to search deep in my memory, fighting my way past the flashbacks blocking my way to find what I had wanted from a father when I was a child. It was a slow and painful process, interrupted by the continuous and hideous images, but both Justin and Lee deserved that I should make a special effort.

I knew I couldn't live up to my own fantasy of the ideal father, but I was determined to get as close as humanly possible. I was happy to get out of bed in the early hours of the day to spend time with either of the boys if they couldn't sleep. It was good to know I could be a comfort to them. Nappies, teeth, bad dreams, were all easy to deal with compared to the arctic region in the middle of my own bed.

When I struggled to get to sleep, I would think about Bob, not knowing if his behaviour was idiosyncratic, or if anyone was capable of it. I wanted it to be particular to him. If it was the case that anyone was capable of behaving like him, I had every right to be scared. I would think of those two angelic faces asleep and safe, and I felt a sort of guilt just thinking anyone could hurt them. I wasn't capable of understanding how anyone would want to.

Day by day I watched in wonder as Justin revealed more and more of his character. I felt it was a privilege to get to know him. Although I could see my own likeness in his little features, I was very much aware that he was his own person. Lee was already talking when Nada and I got together, so it was a different process. I had to interpret what he said, and I had to learn his language as quickly as he was learning mine. With Justin I could follow the evolution of his communication skills from the very first sighs and cries. There were no gaps in my understanding of him. At first a baby is only capable of letting you know either that something is wrong or that it is content. Every parent is in the dark for those first few months. Then almost without realising it, you start to recognise different emotions and needs and, before long, very little is expressed by tears and crying.

I find it amazing how babies and small children have that special and particular warmth and smell. I don't mean the smell of talc, or a dirty nappy. It is that natural smell that adults find so calming, but you remain alert however relaxed you are. I suppose it is nature's way of making sure we don't mess things up whilst in a fit of panic. I can remember on one occasion, when Justin was no more than a few months old, that we noticed something wasn't quite right. His skin started to pale, his breathing was shallow and fast.

We took him to the doctor, who told us it was nothing, but Justin was still restless. I was expecting things to get better, but at home we realised things were not changing, and if anything I feared he was getting worse. I took him back, only to be told I was an over-anxious first-time parent, and that there was nothing wrong with the child. I wanted to believe him; I wanted the doctor to be right. I really wanted nothing more than to know Justin was healthy. The third time, after I had seen Justin's face take on a bluish sort of tinge, the doctor was about to roll his eyes and tell me again there was nothing to worry about.

I was furious because I could see Justin was ill, and no-one was taking any interest in what I had to say. While I was younger, and when I was the subject, I was willing to walk away when no help was offered and my cries were ignored. I could easily cope by myself, and I had survived long enough by my own making. Justin was a tiny child, my responsibility, my son. This was something completely different. From my side of the desk, I grabbed hold of his shirt, and made it clear I wanted to know what was wrong with my son.

Within minutes, I was on my way to the hospital, where as soon as they had a look at him, they decided to keep him in for a week. It turned out to be an infection which was affecting his lungs. They explained that when he recovered, he would be as if it had never happened. As he started getting better, they also told me that if we hadn't brought him in when we had, it could have proved fatal.

I was lucky that I was able to be around my child as much as I wanted, and I don't think I missed anything. I felt the razor-like edge of that first tooth breaking through, relieved I would no longer have to look at plates of mush. No matter what it said on the jar, it still looked like the contents of every other jar of baby food - that is to say as if it had already been eaten once before. I was ten feet tall the first time Justin smiled at me in recognition. I was grinning for days on end the first time he called me Dad. I was so proud of him and pleased with myself when amongst all that babbling I would recognise real words.

I watched him sit up, and fold in on himself instantly, and then each time after, holding out a little longer. It seemed just a matter of days before he was holding himself up, straight back, a huge grin on his face because he saw the world from a new perspective. I was with him when he crawled for the first time, a determined look set on his face. I held his hands as he took his first careful and tentative steps. A little later he would run to me, asking for his potty, and later still he would push me away, sure he could use the toilet by himself. My heart would soar, knowing I was around to see all those little milestones which mean so much, each one proving I was successful in making him independent. He was, all too quickly, becoming his own person.

On his first day at nursery, he seemed so small, and almost as fragile as he had been the day he was born. I was more upset than he was; for him it was a new adventure. It was all so new and exciting. I came to realise I was happy being needed, but Justin wouldn't need me forever. He was learning well, and learning quickly. I was spurred on to be an even better father to him, because I needed him to want me in his life.

I have no choice but to believe that history repeats itself. I have seen more than enough proof over and over again, and unfortunately there is hardly anything you can do about it. My son was the same sort of age as I was when Brenda took me away from my father. The decision wasn't one I made, or considered for any great length of time; separating from Nada was almost impulsively the right thing to do at the time, but I never wanted to separate from Justin. I regret I did not make time to consider what I should tell him, because I know he deserved to hear from me, why I would no longer be a major part of his life.

It was because of incidents like the one that led to my arrest that I began to believe my relationship with Nada was becoming more trouble than it was worth. We had been arguing, and as usual our household items were taking flying lessons. I would have been willing to put up with it; my whole childhood was made up of similar experiences, but I saw no reason why my child, or any child for that matter, should have to watch that. I knew Nada would calm down at some point, so I decided to let her get on with it. I picked up Justin, and took him to a friend where we stayed the night. For Justin it was a nice distraction, and a bit of an adventure. I tried at least to make it a game for him; I felt there was no need for him to worry about what he had seen.

It didn't take long for the police to come by and arrest me. I was gob smacked with the charge. Kidnapping my own child. I thought I was getting him to safety, but the law was such that mothers have right of custody, unless deemed unfit. I hadn't asked for consent to take the child away, and therefore it was to be a charge of kidnapping. The police could see my side of the story. Once I had explained why I took him away, they were satisfied there was no untoward motive. They explained the law, and told me it wasn't something I should consider again. It was still a little insulting to find out that even for a child born in wedlock, the father doesn't have automatic custody.

They let me go and I hoped that, whatever the outcome for me, I would be able to do what I thought to be right and best for my child. Although I understood the concept, I was soon to learn what *inat* looked like, up close and personal. I believed a little distance would give me a better perspective of the situation, I hoped it would be easier to see where we had gone wrong and if there was any way we could rectify the relationship. I wanted the boys to grow up with two parents around. Even if we weren't together, I felt it would have been nice if we both survived to see the boys become adults.

Remembering the kidnapping incident, I wanted Nada's consent on everything. I wasn't willing to take any chances, because being a father, and a good one at that, was important to me. Being a husband was something I feel I was willing to put aside. So I would ask her to tell me when it was best for her to let me have Justin. We would arrange where, when, and for how long we could get together, and nothing. Either Nada wouldn't show up, or she wouldn't bring Justin with her.

The matter even got as far as the courts. It was glaringly obvious to everyone that she was stringing me along, but I wasn't yet willing to give up on being involved with my child. It took several court sittings, frustrating meetings with solicitors, as well as more wasted appointments where we kept missing each other, before I finally admitted I had been worn down into giving up. One of the worst attempts at trying to prove I shouldn't have contact with Justin was when she claimed that while he was with me I wasn't a responsible parent. She tried to claim that on one occasion when he was with me, Justin asked if his cousin David could stay overnight. Nada then went on to say the children were not being adequately supervised. I was upset that the extended family was going to be dragged into this mess.

It felt like a painful defeat. I wanted to be a good parent; I was willing to offer more than I had ever had as a child myself, and for that very reason. It took me a long time to get over my option of parenthood being taken away from me so deftly and, in my eyes, so spitefully.

I knew what this would mean to both Justin and me. I spent hours and hours wondering what he was doing, what he was wearing. I hoped he was well; I wanted him to be happy. It was easy for me to picture him; however fast he was growing, there was one thing that would remain the same. That cheeky smile, that knowing grin everyone recognised as mine would be his as well. Who was helping him with his homework? Who could he talk to if he had a problem?

Did he have any hobbies? I couldn't help but wonder whom he would choose as a role model, who would be his inspiration. Did he remember me, would he think of me? I would wonder what he associated with the word dad. I worried about what it meant to him, what I had meant to him, and if I meant anything to him now.

I tried to imagine what sort of questions he would ask me, if he ever came looking for me. I wanted to be prepared. I couldn't bear the idea that I would put him through what my own father had done to me. It scared me to think that the outcome of such a meeting could be a repeat of the one between David and me. The last thing I wanted was for Justin to come to me for answers and to turn away with nothing but an overwhelming feeling of disappointment.

I knew I had let him down. I hoped some time soon I would have the opportunity to make amends. I would hope, if nothing else, that Justin himself would want to hear my version of events from me. I hoped that if I couldn't be an influence on him throughout his childhood, he would at least grow up to be objective and fair. One day soon, I hoped he would allow me back into his life.

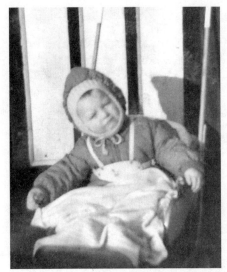

Me (1967)

My brother, Ian

My son, Justin, fishing

Nan Hutchings,
Dad, and Mum

Mum, Nan Hutchings, Ian, Lucy,
and me (kneeling)

Nan Hutchings

Chapter Twelve

A Crossroads

THIS will probably turn out to be a bit of a lesson in philosophy, at least for me. Life speeds past in the blink of an eye, and we do not have the time to ponder all the important questions if we're trying to live it. There are very few moments in a man's life when he has twenty twenty vision and understanding of the world around him. Usually it is just a fleeting moment of focused clarity, where everything makes sense, and the mind is aware of everything as one whole, and as individual concepts.

I have been lucky, or possibly unlucky, to have had just such an experience. Following an argument with Nada, or I should say during, I left the house, and went to get my shotgun. I have no idea what I wanted to do with it, but the options seemed endless. Murder? Suicide? Both? A threat to be able to get a word in edgeways? Who knows?

My mind was like a shed, but at the same time, I was aware of every single individual thought. Do I use the gun? Will firing it calm my frustrations? I doubted it. Yet at the same time I felt that a deafening shot vibrating against my eardrums would dissipate my anger. I knew the noise would shut off her incessant chatter, but with the mood she was in, it was just as likely it wouldn't even phase her.

I had grown used to being a target for knives, plates, cups, even paving slabs, and anything else that would fit into a human hand. Were Bob and Nada kindred spirits? They both threw things with the same passion, eyes blazing with anger. How would the hunter be once he was the prey? It must be nice for the hunted to gain the floor and give chase.

It would serve her right if I shot myself. How far was she willing to push me? If she was playing fair, I would know where the line was, how far I could go before I crossed it. Maybe she didn't know herself, having moved them so often. Or is that what she wants? But maybe I should spite her, and not do it. She wants me out of her way, perhaps I should be a gentleman, and fulfil her wishes one last time. Knowing Nada, she would be angry with me. The electricity bill is still in my jacket pocket and I should have gone to the post office yesterday. Post.

Post. I haven't opened that letter that arrived this morning, probably junk mail, 'you sir, have won loads of money. Send us a tenner and you'll never hear from us again'. Or perhaps it was another bill. I should send one to the other. 'I am about to win loads of money, please feel free to take what I owe you from these people.'

Lee needs new colouring pencils for school. Why am I thinking of what her child needs? The ball of bile builds up, pushing its way up to my throat. She doesn't deserve to have me think of anything that has anything to do with her. I like the child. All this has nothing to do with him. I was happy to be his stepfather. I am angry with me, with Nada, with anyone and everyone who has made me feel this way.

Those clouds look heavy; I'm sure my insides are the same. I think the clouds are just passing; are my feelings just as fleeting? If I am just passing through this world, does it matter when I step off? When it comes down to it, are we not just like all the other animals, eating, breathing, mating, sleeping, killing, dying?

The cheese sandwich I had for lunch was nice - firm cheese, soft bread, and a really crunchy crust. Where did I get that loaf? But that question is immaterial until I decide what I am going to do with the gun. I hate these jeans; I hate the way the waistband folds in on itself when I bend over. The button hides under it, as if that could save it from popping open. Am I getting fat? Do I really care? I'm holding a shotgun in my hands, wanting to decide if I should end my life, and my brain is trying to calculate yesterday's calorie intake.

What is the point of the offside rule? Does anyone know where silly-mid-off is? Why do people fight wars? Who enjoys playing chess? Who invented flares? Why was it that while everyone around me was preaching to make love not war, all I could do was hate? How do you explain natural disasters? Why do people take advantage when all you want to do is help?

Am I stupid? Do I have to prove myself? Should I prove myself to anyone? If I had had any brain I would have done this years ago. Even months ago wouldn't have been too late. What am I waiting for? It's not as if anyone is queuing up to persuade me not to. There's only one thing I'm good for and, since they closed the pits, I can't carry coal around any more.

I don't think anyone sees me as a person, just a useful tool to help get things done, and ignored until later. Brenda was disappointed that I showed my feelings, and Bob was ashamed the neighbours would notice I had emotions. David didn't want to know me at all.

Nada screams at me all the time. What is the point of being just a waste of space? Maybe I'm the one who's got it wrong. Is it possible that all these people around me agree with each other, but have misunderstood me entirely? If I walk away from the gun, then I can be sure they are wrong.

I never jumped from a plane, I never sang out loud. I never tried snake. I can see it clearly in my mind's eye. There's a new cobweb at the top of the stairwell. The spider is crafty and persistent. The web keeps appearing further and further out of my reach. I should admire its ability to start again, yet all I can think of is Nada nagging about how it makes the place look dirty.

It's been ages since I ate a decent roasted pheasant with just a touch of redcurrant sauce and gravy laced with cognac. I wish I could eat a slab of chocolate. No flashbacks, no fears, just chocolate. They say women eat chocolate because it affects the same hormones as sex. I don't understand what is so good about that. Both are overrated. I don't want it for the effects, I just want to be able to do something without the incessant barrage of reminders interrupting my every act. I fancy some pancakes; Sadie often serves them with walnuts, just as Milan used to have them as a child. He used to be a sniper, but I never asked him how much mess you can make from a person when they're close by.

What would I look like after shooting myself? Would the blood trickle out, making my death slow and painful, or would the bullet tear through the flesh, my body in a trance-like state of shock, while it died without me realising. Suddenly I can smell fresh mown grass covered in dew, and an image of Ivan appears before me. He used to give me a good reason to get out of bed in the morning. I wonder where Ison is? He also gave me a reason to avoid my bed. I wonder what it would feel like to put the mouth of the gun against his. Would I have the upper hand? Would he understand my fears, and would he feel what I felt as a child? Why should I be the only one to suffer? Could I pull the trigger? Nestling cold in the crook of my forefinger, just waiting, would it resist my touch, firm and sure, to then relax, before giving me that satisfying click, and bang. It's all over. A bullet is too good for Bob - far too quick. There is one good thing to be said about the speed of a bullet. It should be fast enough to put a stop to those infernal flashbacks. I feel I could punish Bob, but Ison disgusts me; the quicker that matter is finished, the better.

If I put the gun against my temple, would it be instant? Will I forget the flashbacks and the memories of abuse, the memories of long hard beatings? Will I forget that moment when I realised Brenda can't possibly love me? I wish a bullet could work like a delete button. All that bile in my stomach is making me thirsty. If I had a whisky, I would become violent, about as violent as my flashbacks, hard and aggressive, like a rhino pushing at a tree. At least that would lead to some action. At least I would be doing something. This indecision is driving me crazy.

Is there anything worth saving in my life? Am I to blame that Justin has to watch his parents fighting? Should I let her have her way? Will she be happy if we stop fighting? I think maybe she actually enjoys the arguments as much as other people like going out to dinner. Am I too weak, and my only form of defence is attack? Do I only want to hurt others because I can't explain how much I hurt myself? How long have I been holding this gun?

Will anyone notice if I'm not around? Will she have to borrow money to have me buried? Loan rates are high at the moment. I could have opened an account and saved money. Maybe if she pleads poverty well enough, the local council will sort it out. If she's desperate, she can always put me out with the bins on Monday morning. She's bound to resent me for it. Even if she never said it out loud, she would surely think I was being selfish in creating yet another chore for her.

I can smell strawberries; they seem so sweet and close, yet the bile is overpowering. I move the shotgun away from my chest, and it recedes a little. Not enough to ease the burning, just enough for me to notice. I can also smell the gun, cold and hard; the smell is heavy, and it shouldn't be ignored.

I try to have a conscious thought; I have to force myself to think of anything. My brain is like a train that's derailed at high speed. I can't do anything to stop it. A memory of me walking barefoot across a beach. I try to look down; I need to be back in reality, but my eyes refuse to focus. I now realise this state is much like a lucid dream. I am trapped in a whirlwind of my own thoughts as they batter my skull from the inside as if trying to escape.

Nan Hutchings had a nice smile; it was gentle. I wish I could remember what Brenda's smile looked like before it became a mask to cover what she really thought. If David had been around when I was growing up, would I be doing this now? If I go through with it, who would find me? I wonder what the headlines were on this morning's paper - scandal after scandal after scandal. Would they write about me? Cheesed-off Chester chucks it in. Shotgun ends a shitty life. Or would my death be recorded in the small ads? Nagging wife needs cleaner for bloody shed. Calls after last orders only.

What would Justin learn from me? Have I taught him anything useful? Am I any better than the men who tried to be my father? Was I far too damaged to be able to consider anyone else? Was I disappointed that I didn't have a daughter, not instead, as well as, but that would mean making two children suffer. Did I ever think I could make it work with Nada? Did it have anything to do with me anyway?

My bladder aches, I must have been here longer than I first imagined. It's good how nature recycles everything, river, cloud, rain, river, cloud, rain. Is that what will happen to me? Will I be recycled into something better? If I shot anyone else, what would happen to me? I might see that policewoman again - the one with the nice legs who arrested me when I was a kid. I wonder if they have redecorated the cells since I was there last. The paint was chipping. Dark green on top of dark green, and a layer of worn out green showing through as well. Could I plead insanity brought on by continuous torture? 'I'm sorry your honour, I was held hostage by my thoughts, and on top of that I was married to Nada at the time.' That sounds plausible; I could just about get away with it. It makes sense to me.

I have to try to make it clear that these thoughts did not come one after another. I was aware of them all happening at the same time. I held that shotgun for no more than a minute. I know that at that moment in time I knew all the answers to life, the universe and everything, even if I wasn't able to form the concept into words. I realised my thoughts and beliefs were insignificant in the great plan, whoever that belonged to, although I wouldn't be at all surprised to find out it was a Bob-like figure hell-bent on shaping the world with pain. In the great scheme of things, what I thought wasn't important. It was only important to me, and to the way I lived my life. So it was up to me to deal with it.

It was all I could focus on, pain, anger, and a combination of the two. I tried to remember a good time in my life, but to be honest, after that onslaught of ideas in my head it hurt too much trying to focus on anything in particular. I once heard a saying that life is like a bucket of manure with the thinnest of layers of honey at the bottom. If you want to get to the honey, you need to make your way through that bucket. It's crude, but I can't help thinking that the guy who said it must have lived a life similar to mine.

Perhaps becoming aware of those thoughts cleared the way a little, because as I turned back towards the house, it was as if the mists had lifted slightly. I still had all those feelings, but knowing they existed made it a little easier for me to cope with them. I felt as I was at least able to put a name to the face. It was almost as if I had finally recognised my true emotions.

If I were truly honest, I would have to say that all I had gone through during that minute or so while I held the shotgun, is actually academic. None of it matters, because I am still here, still trying to deal with those feelings. I threw some theories about life into the air, and on their way down, they slapped me across the face. All I needed to know was whether or not I was willing to try life again the following day.

That was all it boiled down to. I had had a bad day, and if I wanted to do the right thing for me, I would have to forget about this failed day, and try to make the next a little better. Now how hard could that be?

I had to ask myself if I felt there was any space for love and happiness in my worn and warped mind. I would just have to wait and see.

Chapter Thirteen

Getting On With It

THERE is nothing more painful than coming home to a quiet and empty house. I had been away working, putting a roof onto a barn conversion. I was working a fortnight on, a fortnight off. I was hoping distance and limited communication would ease the strain in our marriage, although deep down I knew it couldn't survive any more. And I returned home to find she had moved the boys out. Nada may have had selected memory recall when it came to whether or not she told me when she was going to move out, but she was certainly thorough when it came to packing.

Like a lingering fragrance, or a fading stain, I could just about picture them around me. Yet in reality, there wasn't a single hint in the house that a child had ever played there. No sign that a family had shared its days between its walls. No plates waiting to smash against the wall, no teddy bear waiting for a cuddle. No radio, no thudding of a ball against the kitchen wall from the garden. The boys' bedtime routine seemed like a distant memory, belonging to the house rather than my own recent past. It was as if I had been alone all my life.

Walking through the house, it felt as if it had been made of paper. There was no substance to it. It mocked me as I walked through each of the rooms, because its existence was as pointless as mine. Yet at the same time I would have been quite happy if it had collapsed onto my head, crushing me and my loneliness. My emotions would lecture me into believing I needed nothing, and deserved nothing, but my brain was still capable of producing practical thoughts, so I knew I didn't have the time to mope. Bills needed paying, and it was looking more and more likely that on top of losing my home, I would also lose the house.

I knew when she left her keys behind that, well, that should have been the end of it. It didn't occur to me to think she may have made a second set for herself. I was too busy nursing wounds, and trying to keep myself occupied to think of changing the locks, so there are bound to be people who think I deserved to come back to find just a shell of a house.

I found myself thinking of my father, David. It wasn't just because I was miserable and that it seemed my whole life was like climbing up a downward escalator, but it seemed more and more that my life was running along the same track as his. Perhaps that was one of the reasons I didn't go looking for him. I was far too disappointed with my life, and I wasn't willing to risk seeing it may not get any better. My father had been in the same sort of situation when Brenda moved away. I grieved as a child because he wasn't a part of our life; I felt he had left me, or, more accurately, that he had let me go.

Having now experienced it for myself, I had to ask 'who abandoned who?' He was the one left with an empty house. As far as I could remember, he had continued taking in lodgers for a while to ease the financial burden, and to overcome the echoes of an empty house as well I should think. I found it was the silence that greeted me in every room, which I hated most of all. It was the haunting emptiness that clings to you as you walk through the door, as if it too needs company.

Before long it would become the only option as I couldn't go back to work. I should say that at the time I thought I wouldn't go back to work, at least not up north where I had been before the split, because the house would be empty and I would be too far away. I didn't want any trouble with people moving in of their own accord, and apart from anything else, I wanted to be close by, so if there was some sort of chance I could have any contact with Justin, I wouldn't miss it.

Not too long after, Fatman asked me to do him a favour by taking in his niece. She was pregnant and had nowhere to stay. Would I mind if she stopped with me while she sorted herself out? Stupid question, I thought, but I let it pass. If someone else was making use of the house as well as me, it might make it feel a little more real. It would make me feel as if I was living something similar to a normal life. Fatman introduced me to Catherine and she moved in. She was happy to share the expenses, so, for a while at least, the bank wouldn't get their hands on my house.

I think both Catherine and I were glad of the company, even though neither of us was willing to risk the suffocation of forced interaction. We would chat about this and that, neither being comfortable enough to get involved in deep and meaningful conversation. She was a shy young thing, kept herself to herself, and let me do as I pleased. I was happy doing nothing, blaming the world and everyone in it that I couldn't be with my son.

I spent more time harassing the solicitor to speed things up, and to get a formal agreement regarding visiting rights, than anything else. I hated the fact that I had to be accompanied by my solicitor when I went to meet with my son, just so we could have it on record whether or not Nada had brought him. Each time she forgot, or had better things to do, or whatever the reason was, I was too angry to care, and all I wanted to know was that I could still have some contact with my child. Another hearing would be booked. The courts are slow, whatever the case may be about. And when it comes to family law, everyone is so careful not to tread on any toes, that the whole thing crawls to a standstill, and is left there 'for the sake of the children'.

I had no time for things like food. It felt like there were days when I wouldn't eat a thing, and then there would be others when I would graze like a sheep, eating anything and everything. Even at the best of times, sleep was not something I would look forward to, so I was happy to wait for exhaustion. My mind would focus on nothing else; I had one task, and one task only. I had to make sure I was still a part of Justin's life.

Of course, I could only manage to focus one part of my mind on anything, because most of it would be fighting with the subconscious in trying to censor and stop the flashbacks and memories flooding through. Some of the associations would seem trivial, but they would be strong enough to be a trigger for an image that would not only stop me in my tracks, leaving me breathless and frightened, but the flashbacks were becoming more frequent the more upset I got.

It felt as if I was in the eye of the storm, and the storm was about to implode just above my head. A vicious circle that was getting tighter as it squeezed around my neck. The more I was fighting my way through the chaos, the more the flashbacks would overwhelm me. It is not just difficult to deal with remembering awful images, but each time the body would react physically to the image, as if it was happening for the first time.

It was as if the warning mechanism in my brain had gone into overdrive. Any time I felt I was in danger, or suffering a negative emotion, the flashbacks were more vivid, stronger than reality. Like a faulty car alarm that is set off by the lightest touch - screeching and wailing until someone switches it off. The only problem was I could never find the off switch.

I knew I needed to keep myself busy; I didn't want to be left alone with my thoughts. My friends were happy to join me if I wanted to drown my sorrows. Some were telling me I should be celebrating a lucky escape. In fact I had never seen so many people trying to urge me to get out of the house. It was as if they all thought I could sort myself out by having a busy social life, even though I was happy being busy by myself. They all thought they would make the ideal distraction. I just couldn't be bothered. I didn't want to be pushed into anything; I needed to make the decision myself.

As far as I was concerned, I was out more often than I liked. I just couldn't feel comfortable around others. I still found it almost suffocating to be amongst others when I didn't have to be. At least if I was at home I wouldn't be caught off guard when I stumbled through the after-effects of a flashback. Although I hated being on my own when it happened, that was easier to cope with than trying to explain why I had been completely blank, almost as if unconscious, or why I was sweating in a cold room. Often I would just be staring into the middle distance, longing to return to the conversation I was a part of mere seconds before.

Without realising it, some people would intrude at the worst possible moment because they wanted to help. It is almost impossible to recognise where and when in the flashback I am furthest away from reality, and therefore when I am most likely to react to the memory rather than to what is happening to me really. It is difficult to say why I feel like that, especially as I know they do it with good intentions, but it is possibly due to the fact that their presence doesn't seem real; they are like a mirage, visible, audible, but my mind is telling me, untouchable. If I try, it seems to me that person will just disappear as if they were a ghost.

So there I was, yet again being manhandled out of my own front door. As always, my mates knew better than I did what was good for me. I'm sure that more often than not I was too close to the action to know which way I should turn; sometimes it is a good thing to let others show you your situation from their perspective. Obviously this is an afterthought, but at the time, everyone thinks they know best, and others are just interfering. Even if I wasn't a willing participant in their night out, they would force me to join them. I made a compromise. I wouldn't grumble, but I wouldn't try to enjoy myself either. If they asked, I would tell them they should be happy I showed. It seemed like a big enough effort for me, and I did it more to get them off my back than anything else. So we stood about, drinking quickly, waiting impatiently for it to take effect, because standing around thinking of all the subjects you must avoid talking about is quite stressful.

I guess it is an English quirk that people have long and detailed conversations about the shallowest and most meaningless of subjects because mentioning a taboo would be insulting to the others, and apart from anything else, if you were meant to find out personal information about someone, they would volunteer it. This of course has nothing to do with the universally known gossip trait found in all strands of DNA; the English just make a better pretence of its absence in normal everyday conversation. This is why our every conversation starts with a question about the weather - impersonal, shallow, and of no consequence.

I stood there, trying to think of nothing, or something; it didn't matter, either was a strain. When, out of the corner of my eye, I caught sight of something - a movement, a smile, a hint of familiarity - I looked for it again, but it had disappeared. I wasn't sure what I was looking for, but I waited while the crowd parted to reveal Helen.

She was carrying a couple of glasses, and deep in conversation with someone. I nudged Wally, making his glass tilt dangerously in his hand. He was about to get upset, I'm sure, and then he noticed I wasn't looking at him. My line of sight was fixed, and he followed it, first to the bar, and then he looked a little further out. He spotted her.

'You watch. I'll marry her one day.'

He was about to laugh when he realised I was serious. He must have thought I was mad. The lighting was bad, the room was smoky, the noise was such that you had to concentrate if you were going to have a proper conversation. The floor was thumping to some rhythm where the bass had worked up to such a speed that it had evolved into a subtle and sublime rumble. And after my last choice of wife, was I really to be trusted in making such a decision by myself?

I didn't blame him if he thought all that and more. Remembering all the effort he and the others made in trying to stop me from making a mistake the last time, he was right to feel this relationship of mine could be a lot of hard work for them. I was so sure of myself and of what was about to happen. But what I had said surprised me. It was as if the decision had nothing to do with me, as if a higher force had shown me who was going to be in my future.

I didn't know then that she was called Helen. But I wasn't at all surprised when I found out her name. She seemed the sort of woman who would cause a stir. I was thinking about how to start up a conversation, when Wally and the others decided we should go over the road to the Co-op club as they had organised karaoke sessions for every Monday and Thursday. I cursed myself for my lack of courage to speak to her, but as the boys were deciding, I followed. We got to the door, and I realised she was standing behind us in the queue. I must have said something corny like, 'you following us, or what?', and she smiled. It was that moment when I realised she was beautiful. Not just strikingly beautiful, in a supermodel kind of way; Helen isn't a two-dimensional image of beauty. She is a beautiful looking woman, tall and graceful, whose inner beauty radiates brightly and makes her a wonderful person to be with.

We were stopped at the front of the queue, only to be told we couldn't go in because we weren't members. I was disappointed, and I thought that would be the end of it. As I turned around, Helen said she and her mates would sign us in as guests. They were allowed one guest each, so we were all covered. The very least we could do was get them a couple of drinks. When men think they may be in with a chance, they start to show off. I was no different. I never sang, well, even when I did sing to myself I would cringe when I heard it. But I allowed Wally to persuade me to do a duet with him. I was thinking, even if she isn't impressed with my singing, at least she'll see I'm willing to join in and have a laugh. Within thirty seconds of our duet starting, the whole club was in hysterics. There wasn't a dry eye in the house. Wally had picked one of those lovey-dovey songs. In order not to offend my masculinity, he chose to sing the female vocals. So there we stood, making eyes at each other, me nervous, Wally revelling in the attention. From the crowd that is, not from me. He'd had his eye on Helen's friend Debbie. Maybe it's just my imagination, but there seemed to be a lot of Debbies about.

It wasn't until a little later that someone mentioned Wally had been singing the part normally sung by Dolly Parton. I found that hilarious; Wally is tall and sinewy with a gaunt face, the sort of man who turns sideways and disappears from sight, and Dolly, well, she's all boobs and vocal chords. Helen enjoyed our attempt at entertainment. The conversation between the two of us flowed so naturally, it was as if we had known each other for years. I was glad that she was far from agreeing with everything I said. The last thing I wanted was a lapdog. Even my mates had worked out I didn't want to be surrounded by yes-men. I preferred reality, however difficult it was, compared to the fantasy they could have created around me.

What I liked most of all was the fact that, when I talked, she listened as if she was interested. Helen made every effort to make me feel comfortable in her company, but it took me a long time to recognise that, in actual fact, I would have to become comfortable being me, in my own skin. When she asked me to sing with her I was sure she was a glutton for punishment, but, even so, I didn't want to disappoint her. As the evening died down, we went our separate ways, but not before agreeing to see each other the following week.

Looking back, that week went by at the speed of light, but living it seemed to take for ever. I knew I had been right; I knew she was the one. I wondered if I were to tell her that, would she run? Would she think I'm too eager? Deep down I knew no matter how long it took, we would get together. I thought about how to tell her what I felt she needed to know.

I didn't want to get into a relationship, only to be told later that I had withheld information. I wouldn't have been able to live with myself if she'd ever thought I had conned her into getting involved with me. Whether I liked it or not, my past was influencing my present, so it was also going to be affecting my future. How do you tell someone you were abused? How do you tell someone, that for most of your childhood, slaps and punches rained around your head, and you had no escape from it?

How would I react, if I was on the other side of the conversation? I had to consider whether or not she would still accept me. It had to be her decision; it would have been selfish and unfair of me to make the decision for her. I wanted her to see me as a normal person who has been through an abnormal experience. There were times in my life, when of course I did wonder if I could ever be a normal person, but just having a quick glance through the newspaper put my fears to rest.

I sat in that same pub where I had met her the week before. The appointed hour came and went. The minutes past, the hour dragged, my whole life flashed as a series of images, each one with the word failure stamped across it. The last one in the cycle was an image of me looking at the clock. Just before I started to believe this propaganda my brain was torturing me with, the door creaked open and a slim shadow slipped past it. I recognised her beautiful smile long before I saw the face. I looked at the clock again - it was only seven minutes past - she was just a little late. There was nothing to get worked up about.

From then on, the date was something like a scene from a film. I kept wanting to pinch myself to be sure I wasn't dreaming, but I stopped myself before Helen had a chance to think of me as weird. That evening we talked. I told her about my childhood, and why I was working so hard to continue being a good father.

Helen told me she understood why Justin was so important to me, because she was a mother of five. She also explained that for quite some time she had been looking for a way out of her relationship. This was on a strictly personal level. She was happy with her partner's relationship with her children, and they had never complained about him to her. For some reason Helen couldn't understand, this man who made such an effort with and for the children, would treat her like something to be scraped off the bottom of his shoe. She couldn't fathom out why he was chipping at her self-esteem. She had made the commitment to be with him, and she saw no reason for him to keep her trapped, financially, as well as emotionally.

My first reaction to what she told me was to say, 'why are you with a selfish moron when you deserve better?' But the expression, 'a pot calling the kettle black' sprang to mind. How could I comment on anyone else's relationship when memories of my life with Nada still burned on the inside of my eyelids? People asked me why I stuck it out with her for so long. I wanted to ask Helen the same thing, but, like myself, I was sure she didn't want to be reminded of her blatant mistakes. From the outside looking in, it is really difficult for people to see why someone won't or can't leave a bad relationship. The barriers aren't always put into place by the other partner, and sometimes the very same barriers are just fear and insecurity, anger and indecision.

I had to admire her objectivity. I struggled with my emotions, yet Helen was and is capable of detaching herself from the situation, and seeing it with new eyes. I loved the fact that she would keep calm before making a decision. We were both aware of the fact that this wasn't just a case of lust turning our heads, and that in the cold light of day we wouldn't be able to look each other in the eye, or anyone else for that matter. It was the real thing. I realised from early on that she had a bit of an adventurous streak. There was no food she wasn't willing to try. In fact, when I asked her if she had a favourite, she wasn't able to decide if she had one.

When I told her about what had happened to me, there was just the tiniest of shrugs. It wasn't that she didn't care, she was simply letting me know that it didn't matter, and it wasn't going to affect her wanting to get involved with me. Had I not been seated, I would have been floating on a cloud.

From the very first moments of the relationship, Helen and I were frank and honest with each other. Having both been lied to, we knew it was something we wanted to avoid. And we started as we meant to go on. We talked; she was the first person I felt comfortable with. Helen allowed me to be myself, and she didn't judge. She often had an opinion, but I was never made to feel as if my mine was not worth any consideration.

On the way out of the pub, I told her I could give her a lift in the Ferrari. I wasn't sure if she believed me, but I had the feeling that, even if it was a joke, she was willing to go along with it. As we stepped outside, Helen looked around the car park, and there was nothing there that would even barely resemble a car, let alone the red icon of Italian style. As I walked over to the works van, I heard a groan behind me. Suddenly, I saw the shattered front windows, the paint pots and tools strewn in the back, as if with her eyes. I shuddered, but she caught up with me, and I knew, from that moment on, we would be inseparable.

I gave her some time to decide what she was going to do about her relationship with the man she was with before. Yet as far as I was concerned, if she was willing, our life's journey together had already started.

We were glued at the hip. Even going to the corner shop to get the local paper, we would go together. Helen and I would walk through the park, hand in hand, just enjoying listening to our breaths fall in sync with each other. Helen was struggling to overcome her feelings about leaving her children with their father. She knew they would be safe, and provided for, and although my intentions were honourable, I couldn't tell if I would have a roof over my head this time next week, so I tried not to influence her decision. I kept telling her that whatever she had to do, she would have my support.

The two youngest were all for their mother having a new and better relationship. They wanted her to be happy, and they didn't get to see that at home. The older children were weary; Lindsey especially was set against it. She believed it was far too disruptive for the family unit. She didn't want her mother rocking the boat. She felt that with five children, there was too much at stake. Helen and I both thought it was just a fear of the unknown. With time, as she got to know me, and as she distanced herself from the environment her mother had been in before, she became a little more objective about it. Before too long, we became friendly, and she saw me and my relationship with her mother in a positive light.

Helen moved in with me, and Catherine was still in the house. I didn't realise I should have read all the small print on the mortgage contract. One of the conditions was that sub-letting isn't allowed. I knew plenty of people who got away with something like that, and I got the feeling it was common practice for those who were trying anything to stay in their own homes.

Nada had been a little more vigilant. I was struggling with the payments because she had emptied the accounts. She left me with no choice but to refuse my only reasonable source of income if I wanted any contact with my son, and then, as if all that hadn't been enough, she reported me for misuse of property to the bank.

Before they could do anything about it, Catherine's health took a turn for the worse. Helen was at home with her; they were just talking when Catherine got up and told Helen something wasn't right. Helen could see that she was distressed, and wanted to help, but before she was able to do anything, Catherine started to miscarry. Helen called me to let me know what had happened, and went to the hospital with the poor girl. She seemed too young at nineteen to be going through such a harrowing time. They kept her in the hospital for two weeks, and her family picked her up to take her home. If I could have avoided making that phone call, I would have, but I felt, because she had been living in my house, that it was my responsibility to keep them informed.

I got into the habit of leaving notes and cards for Helen to find, anywhere from her pillow to the fridge. Nothing too artistic, more along the lines of roses are red, violets are blue... but genuine all the same. I tried to show her how much she meant to me by preparing meals for her, and getting her settled in front of the coal fire in the evenings. I wanted her to know that, while she was with me, she could relax and be herself. Even if we weren't spending money on each other, I made sure she could have something tangible to prove our relationship was real.

The money situation was changing drastically, but for the worse. The bank was sending polite but threatening letters. The bills were piling up and, however much I knew Helen was missing her children, it would have been foolish to have them with us. If the worst came to the worst, it would be better if two people were homeless than seven.

In the end, when I had had enough, I told Helen I was going to put an end to it. I asked her to start looking for somewhere to live while I sorted this mess out. I picked up the last in a long series of letters from the bank, and went to see the manager. I wanted to know if we could come to some sort of compromise, but it was clear from the very beginning of the conversation, that I would not be able to have my say. I took out my house keys, and dropped them on the desk.

'Take them, they belong to you anyway.'

I heard him start to say something about things being done the right way, but I was on my way out before he had finished the sentence. I was sick and tired of having to listen to everyone else telling me how things should be done. No-one had shown any interest in what I wanted. It felt as if everything was outside of my control. I was determined to do something about it. Relinquishing the keys was probably the easiest thing I had ever done. The build-up to it was hard, slow and painful, yet hearing the keys hit the desktop, was a nice sound. It was my decision; it was what I wanted to do at the time.

I knew that with Helen by my side, no obstacle would prove too hard. Even if it wasn't yet in sight, I knew the light at the end of the tunnel really did exist. Some evenings, all we did was sit in front of the television. I was finally happy to have someone close to me. I expected to compare her to Nada, even if it was just to reaffirm Helen couldn't be better if she tried, but now that I was with her, nothing and no-one else mattered. I understood why some people floated down the street, with a huge grin taking over their face. I could now smile at them knowingly. I too am loved.

All those songs I didn't give a second thought to before suddenly made sense. Yes, I think I can fly without ever leaving the ground; it is the butterflies in my stomach that lift me into the air. They start with a little flutter because just as I start to wake up, I know she is the first thing I see. And they don't stop until I get to sleep again.

I knew Helen felt the same way, because she would look at me, and it would feel like a caress. She would turn to kiss me, and it would feel as if every single cell in my body had jumped with a surge of electricity, and for the shortest of moments I was aware of each individual cell; then just as quickly, they would adhere to each other again, and I would feel whole.

No matter what I was doing, she was willing to join in. Helen didn't mind metal detecting, but I know she thought all those coins and indeterminate pieces were boring. The only time I saw her get excited was when I found that brooch. Even so, she walked all those miles, so I knew she liked my company.

We used to go fishing often, and Helen's brother would join us sometimes. I had the feeling that Helen was at peace with herself. She was happy just sitting nearby, knowing the silence didn't have to be filled, but perhaps it was just the appreciation of silence when she heard it. We had moved into rented accommodation, a flat next to a pub.

Sounds great, you don't have to go very far to go out for a drink, and if you've had one too many, you certainly don't have to worry about how you're going to get home. When we first saw it, it didn't seem too bad. What we didn't realise was that, although a pub is quiet first thing in the morning, as the day passes, the noise gets progressively louder until you think the only way to drown out the noise is to fall into a drunken stupor. By midnight, all would be quiet again. Although Helen could get to sleep, the dark and quiet was an open invitation for all my demons to start their onslaught.

Even though things were difficult, I was in love and happy. I had more than enough reason to feel frustrated and angry. In fact, my life was falling apart. Helen gave me a reason to keep trying. I wanted to succeed because of her. It was obvious to me, and everybody else, that we were meant to be together. There was one thing left to do, and that was to make our commitment official.

We got married at a registry office. On that December afternoon I only saw Helen's smile and I knew it was for me. There were other people around, but I was only vaguely aware of them. I heard plenty of background noise, but I couldn't recognise individual voices. At that moment, all my mistakes seemed to be trivial; all my hardships over. I knew when Helen signed her name for the first time as Mrs Chester, everything would be all right.

Chapter Fourteen

At the Bottom Looking Up

WE HAD settled into some semblance of routine and, although life was difficult, both Helen and I felt that we were making progress. Kim, Helen's youngest, came to live with us, and the older four would visit us regularly. They were all now a part of my life, and I hoped they would appreciate my presence in a positive light. We made time to do things as a family, and we made time for each other. It was hard work trying to fit into a family, especially when they are all so loving and close. I did worry that Helen's children would consider my relationship with her as an intrusion on their time with their mother. Yet they accepted me pretty quickly. It took me a bit of time to learn who liked what and how they interacted with each other.

Just as an example of this, I can remember being quite shocked, when walking in on a conversation, to hear the children talk about Helen, using the name rather than calling her Mum. It would take me a moment to work out they were actually discussing their eldest sister, also called Helen. In time I learnt to recognise that Helen was always called Mum, and that they had made this distinction a long time ago.

The girls are loud as individuals, and even louder when they get together, none of them allowing either of the other two to get a word in edgeways. Alan, the oldest boy and middle child, is the quietest, talking more or less only when someone demands it of him. Chris is quite similar to Alan, in that he seems very shy, until of course he is anywhere near his younger sister Kim.

Kim is a determined young girl, who, with the confidence of pre-puberty, knows that she is right, and will defend her opinions to the last. Chris, at just fifteen months older is the proverbial red rag. To Helen and me it seems that they have been having the same argument for the last two years. I asked Helen once if there was anything we could do about it because I hated to see them fight. She just rolled her eyes heavenward and told me they would grow out of it. Helen and Lindsey did. Lindsey and Alan did. They're all close now, so we have to be patient.

Coping with up to five or even six different breakfasts when any or all of the other siblings were visiting, as well as a school run, before allowing your own day to start, was daunting, but both Kim and Chris made it more of an adventure than a chore. I was happy to be accepted in a parental role. I guess I felt, and still feel, I could learn from, and do better than the parents and upbringing I'd had. Even though it was more or less new to me, I loved being a part of a family, where each member was valued, and the whole family unit is worth more than the sum of its constituent parts.

At the time of writing, Helen junior has a boy and a girl, with another one on the way, but because she lives a little further away we get to see them about once a fortnight. We get to see Lindsey and her son Morgan every weekday because he comes to us after nursery while his mum is at work. Alan is in a stable long-term relationship, and they're all relatively happy.

I was happy for Helen who was in a loving and stable relationship; her children supported her and us, and once again they are part of her life. She deserved that much and more. I don't, and never have, begrudged anyone their happiness, especially someone I love as much as Helen, but I did resent having my rights as a natural father ripped from me. It was even more painful when I thought it was done on a spiteful whim.

I wanted the chance to be as happy with my own child as I was with my stepchildren. In the short time I had spent with them, I felt I had more than enough reason to be proud of them all. I hoped that one day they would be able to look at me in the same positive light.

I thought that even if the good and bad things in my life were about equal on the scales, then I would be able to cope. After all, I had lived through times when there was nothing good in my life, so surely being with Helen, and helping her with her children, should balance things out? It wasn't to be. For days, perhaps even weeks, all I could focus on was what I was missing and why I no longer had my son in my life. Each day I would struggle to focus on the good things that were happening in my life.

Then the day came when I'd had enough. My brain, as if in worry overdrive, decided simply to go on strike. I hadn't realised it at the time, but looking back I think that is the only way to describe what had happened.

I had been fishing the whole day. Helen was with me, as was her brother Jeff, and the time passed quietly. Jeff and Helen used to join me on my fishing expeditions, and we would be out for up to fourteen hours a day, and anything up to four times a week. Sometimes I would change my colleagues, and I would go fishing with Helen's brother-in-law Len. He was a passionate fisherman, much like me. He used to talk about the one fish he wanted to catch before he died. He was after a twelve pound barble, a rare fish, mostly talked about over a pint, but rarely seen hanging from a hook. Sadly, Len is no longer with us, but he fulfilled his dream, and I was proud to be with him when he reeled it in.

That day, I seemed to be lost in thought, when in actual fact my brain felt as if it had been replaced by cotton wool. It was as if my thoughts were trying to wade through water. Everything felt like a struggle, even looking at something was an effort.

It had been hot and sunny, but I kept to the shade. It wasn't that I particularly wanted to remain my usual pasty, almost clammy, colour, but my flashbacks tend to be stronger, and the images clearer, in daylight. I try to avoid all known triggers, so when I know I'm going to be outside for any length of time, I plan for most eventualities. Armed with a hat and plenty of shade, I spent the day covered up.

I had done nothing out of the ordinary, except maybe catch three fish one after the other in quick succession. By mid-afternoon, I was sweating and shivering, running hot and cold all over. We headed back home. I was so thirsty that I just couldn't get enough water into me. I dragged myself into bed, and withdrew from the world.

For days on end, all I could do was sleep. Like a tiny baby, I would wake up every four hours or so, just to open my eyes and close them again. I don't remember turning over or changing position. Helen called the doctor, insisting on a home visit, because it was obvious there was something wrong. She was dismissed with the explanation that it was sunstroke, and nothing more.

My brain was still mush. During that time, while I just lay there, I could think nothing nor feel anything. It was as if my nerve endings had been wrapped in bandages to protect them, and that everything was muted.

None of the senses seemed to be in focus. I was aware of a heavy, yet hollow sensation, but it was only later that I came to realise that what I was feeling was actually my body. I seemed incapable of movement. I was too big and too heavy to move from the inside. My thoughts weren't strong enough to initiate anything, let alone a recognisable movement.

Whilst sleeping, I had no sense of time or space. I would open my eyes, and try to focus on my surroundings. I was aware of the room I was in, but nothing more than that. I didn't care where I was; I didn't know if the room was mine, but it wasn't even important, at least not until I had proper periods of wakefulness. As I started to remain awake for longer than two minutes at a time, the room became the most important thing to me.

I didn't want to leave the room, or even move around it. It was cool and dark, and most of all it was calm. There was nothing busy in there, nothing screaming for my attention. The whole room was bland, and everything would blend into one concept, me included.

Even on a gloomy day, the sun was far too bright, and it hurt my eyes. There was no other option but for the curtains to remain closed. Without the sunlight tearing at my retinas, I felt safer and more cocooned. I tried to remember what food had tasted like before. All that would do was give me a headache, because it felt like I was searching for something that didn't exist. I wanted to make an attempt at eating because I assumed I must be hungry, but no sooner had some food reached the bottom of my stomach, it would come straight back up again.

The sheets needed changing twice a day because of the amount of sweat I was producing. It was like one of those dolls that pee when you give them water, except that, as I swallowed the water or Lucozade, it would pour out of my skin. I needed something different from water, and as I wasn't holding down any food, Lucozade was the only thing I thought of to help me get through this. I could vaguely remember drinking it as a child because my grandmother used to give it to me so I could get better quicker.

I hated the intrusion almost as much as the cold wet sheets clinging to my skin. Helen would come in with a fresh set of bedding, and I would have to get out of bed. Standing up, waiting for Helen to finish seemed like ever such a long time. I was cold, and unprotected from the elements. It felt like there was constantly someone behind me, and I was waiting for them to grab me by the shoulder. I had a muggy, smudged sensation, which I later recognised as desolation, isolation, and despair.

I would be standing there, shivering and shaking. I was fearful. I was cold. I had an overwhelming urge to cry. I couldn't recognise my source of fear, yet it was almost solid, a real and tangible thing I wasn't yet able to locate. Although Helen tried to help, I wasn't able to explain to her what she may be able to do in order to help me out. I just wanted to be back in my bed. Wrapped up underneath the blankets, I was warm and safe. Nothing could get to me, for a little while at least.

In time, I started to notice the noise from outside the room. It would seep in, almost unnoticed, filling every last inch of space, before it smothered me. I needed to escape it; I needed to stop it coming in. Outside the door, there was noise, and the source of the fear as well. Of course it would be safer for me to deal with it from inside the room, and even better from under the covers. It scared me; it was intrusive and aggressive. I didn't know how to block it out. I wanted to stop it somehow, but my brain couldn't comprehend the situation, never mind find a solution. It was almost screaming at me, 'there's too much noise for me to function; you can't expect me to work under these conditions!'

I asked Helen to bring the television and video into the bedroom. So all day long I would try to concentrate on what was on the screen. For the most part, it served as white noise, something in the background to drown out the noise from outside the room. I would start to watch a film and, without noticing, I would drop off to sleep, and wake up a little later, completely unaware of the lapse in time. Looking back, it now makes perfect sense why I thought all those films were bad. I'd missed most of the plot lines for any of them to make sense.

My sleep was becoming fitful once again. At regular intervals during the day, I would get an overwhelming urge to cry. I didn't know why I was grieving, or even what I was grieving for, I just knew the pain was unbearable; I was sure I would never get over it. I wanted to sob, but usually nothing happened. When the floodgates finally opened and the tears flowed, I wasn't even aware of what was going on. When it was over, I only felt a sense of relief wash over me.

I can remember nothing except seeing Justin in my mind's eye, and his big wide grin when he saw a chocolate bar peeking out of my jacket pocket. I heard his sigh, and turned around expecting to see him as he was when he was a baby, content just after a feed. I saw his face, at the age of three, almost cross-eyed with concentration, his tongue following one end of a lace, as I showed him how to tie it.

I would lie there trying to picture my grandmother. As a child she would give me Lucozade to drink, and lots of cuddles when I wasn't well. It felt that whatever was wrong, she knew how to put it right. And it would all start with that sparkling energising drink. I knew I would have to persevere, and that with a bottle of Lucozade in my hand, no matter how long it took, I was sure to get better.

I tried to picture her, but her image wouldn't come to me. I could feel myself sinking deeper and deeper into what felt like a self-inflicted depression. The one person who was there for me at the worst of times, the one who was a shoulder to cry on whenever I needed it, I now couldn't summon from my memory. It was as if I had betrayed her and everything she had ever done for me. At that moment, I despised myself for not even attempting to pull myself out of it. Later on, I realised it was a natural process, and I had to drop to the very bottom before I could see the way out at the top.

The first time I tried to get out of the room was an absolute nightmare. Just the thought of it seemed to have me shrinking back into the bedding. I felt the fear had become a physical sticky substance which kept me glued in place. As I pulled the covers back, my whole body started to shake in protest at being moved from the only recognisable place of safety. I walked like a toddler, not at all sturdy, with my legs giving way just as I got to the next piece of furniture, and grabbed on hoping it was just a dream. I hoped that, when I woke up, I would be safe under the covers. I looked back to see the empty bed, and I wanted to think of the progress I had made, but all I could think was how far away my only sanctuary was.

By the time I had seen the staircase, I was sure I would vomit. Thankfully my stomach was empty, so that nothing came up as my guts wrenched themselves as if they too wanted to escape the fear filling my body. I sat down on the top step, finding the stair carpet unusually rough on the backs of my thighs. I had spent so long on cotton sheets that I felt I would be incapable of feeling anything else.

They seemed so steep, and at first glance there were so many I couldn't possibly count them. I dropped one foot onto the next step, just to get a feel of it. It was steep, dropping into the abyss of the ground floor. Yet it was also fluid, like my foot was sinking into it. I was certain it couldn't possibly hold my weight. I thought I was going to topple over, bouncing off each step, knowing that by the time I got to the bottom I would never know how many there are. The fear of falling slowly subsided, but returned again instantly as I tried again with the other foot.

Both feet together, I slid my behind to the edge of the first step. My head was too far forward, and I was going to overbalance and fall for certain. One deep breath, two deep breaths, and a third one just to make sure. Still playing that balancing game at the top of the stairs, I decided to take the plunge. My hands next to my hips, I pushed myself along, letting my pelvis drop on to the next step down.

This was progress. But it was like watching a flower grow. It would be fine if the film was speeded up. I hated myself. I had to believe I would make it to the bottom. I knew I needed to leave the room, but I also knew I didn't want to. Each thud on the next step sent a reassuring shudder through my tired and wasted body. By the sixth or seventh step, I decided to stand up. Perhaps then I wouldn't seem so small; maybe I would even get a better perspective of the size of the hallway. From where I was, it must have been about thirty feet high. The staircase seemed to be crowding me, getting narrower the further it dropped away from me.

By the time I had made it to the foot of the stairs, the whole hallway took on its old dimensions again. Each door I tried to push open would resist, almost telling me I was unwelcome. My brain was screaming at me, danger, fear, get back. I knew I needed, and wanted, to be back in my own bed.

The days dragged on, and all I had managed to do was to extend my boundaries of safety. I was now able to walk shakily around the house, enjoying, most of all, being able to use the bathroom by myself. The first time I locked the door behind me, I felt the exact opposite of what I had been feeling everywhere else. All of a sudden I was closed in, smothered by the walls creeping in on me. Once I had opened the door, it felt like the agoraphobia from minutes before had smacked me in the face, knocking me back into the bathroom. I gulped some air, trying hard not to vomit the fear that had appeared out of nowhere. The click of the door handle had been the trigger. I knew that if I was going to make my way out of these fears I was going to have to commit to memory anything that could be a trigger.

I didn't dare peek into a mirror; I knew I looked nothing like the man I used to be. My skin felt loose, and I was aware I had lost a lot of weight, but had no idea how much until I stepped on the scales to see that I was just over four stones lighter than I had been on that last fishing trip. I needed a shave and a good meal. I didn't feel up to either. That would have to wait until tomorrow, or the next time I made an attempt to get out of my room.

I could live with my fears, pushing them deep down, hiding them, crushing them into the tiniest space, hoping they wouldn't burst open or leak as they had after that fishing trip. I realised it was a show of grief I hadn't dealt with earlier. I missed my Justin; I missed my grandmother. I missed not having my parents to comfort me. I missed waking as a happy child; I missed restful sleep. I now missed Helen; I was scared, and she was out there, living.

I had to make the choice.

Chapter Fifteen

From Bad to Worse

ALL I CAN say is that the last month had been a bad one. Lindsey was spending more and more time with us. She lived close by, and baby Callum enjoyed looking at the world around him from his buggy. Lindsey would just be sitting there, silently watching her only child playing by her feet. Callum was a cute baby, all cheeks, bright eyes and smiles. I felt lucky that I had been around since the birth, and was a part of his life from the very beginning.

He used to gurgle at me when I blew raspberries on his belly button, and while he was around, I managed to forget that I had once held my own child in the same way, and lost him. I hoped and prayed we could all enjoy and savour our time with him. He was a happy child, and quiet too. He would never complain too much, unlike his mother. Helen would never grow tired of telling Lindsey how much trouble she had been as a baby. She used to be shipped out to an aunt at the weekend, just so Helen could get some sleep. It wasn't that she cried, Helen would say, it was the whining, the closest thing to complaining from a baby not yet talking. It was an annoying noise, a miserable bleating as if she knew exactly what the world was like and she didn't like it.

Lindsey was obviously having problems in her relationship, and normally she would be happy to set the record straight within the family environment. Lindsey is the sort of person who wouldn't keep quiet when she felt she had to say something, but this was something she didn't want to talk about even though she knew we had realised what sort of relationship she was in.

I could empathise with her; after all I was only too aware of the signs of an abusive relationship. I was worried about what Callum was having to see, knowing Lindsey was doing everything possible to make sure he didn't see anything too upsetting. I knew, because I had done that exact same thing for my own child. I understood completely how she felt having to lie and hide, from herself as much her child, as well as everyone else.

Any time the subject came up, she would pretend to be in denial, because that was easier than admitting she had a failed relationship. It was obvious that even she didn't believe what she was saying; it was just a polite way of telling us to keep out of it. I wanted desperately to tell her it wasn't her who had failed. Failure and blame must lie at the hands of the abuser. She needed to know, even though it was still considered a taboo subject, that it was no sign of weakness to ask for or to accept help. Lindsey's way of showing she was strong enough to deal with it was to refuse all offers of help.

Every time she went back home, we prayed we would hear from her the next day. We wanted to be able to tell her the relationship was doing damage to both her and Callum. No matter how hard she tried, it was impossible for her to hide everything from a toddler. He was a bright and friendly child, inquisitive too. I wouldn't have been surprised if, as soon as he started speaking, he would start asking questions.

We loved, and I especially loved, being with him, and to be honest it was unusual that we didn't or couldn't look after him when Lindsey wanted. That afternoon, Lindsey called to ask us if we could take him for the evening. Helen had agreed with some friends to go to the bingo for the first time in months and, just before she arrived, a friend of mine called to say he wanted to meet up.

I was just about comfortable again doing the things I used to do before the breakdown, so I was keen to start socialising again for my own benefit more than anything else, but I also felt I needed to give Helen some space. She had spent so much time with me, waiting patiently for me to begin the recovery process, she deserved for me to get out from under her feet. I was happy for her to go out, and when my friend called, I thought it might be better if I was with someone rather than be alone at home.

So when Lindsey called, we had to tell her we were busy. We were a little down because we didn't like to refuse Lindsey any help, especially knowing that she was working, rather than wasting time and money just to enjoy herself. We genuinely liked having Callum with us, but we also needed to have some time to our selves.

So that evening, Callum was left in the care of Pilch, a man also known as Richard Plender. He was Lindsey's boyfriend at the time. He claimed Callum had sustained his injuries by falling down the stairs, and would not admit any responsibility for what had happened. All he would finally admit was to leaving eleven-month-old Callum alone in his cot while he went to buy a lottery ticket.

I got back home, and even before I turned the key in the lock I had a bad feeling in the pit of my stomach. I dialled 1471; the last number that had called in wasn't registered. I put the phone down, and picked it up again as it rang before I had the chance to let it go. The pit of my stomach churned; I wasn't sure I was willing to have the conversation that was about to follow.

At first I thought it was a joke. A voice I didn't recognise was telling me I needed to go to the hospital because Callum had died. Before I had a chance to say anything they put Lindsey on the phone, and even before she uttered a word, just hearing her gulping back the sobs, I knew it was true. I knew if she ever needed me, it would be now. I didn't dare consider my own feelings; I was the least important one in all this.

I looked around, and wondered where to start. What would I need to do? First of all, Helen needed to know. I jumped into the car, and went looking for her. I'm sure, as soon as she saw my face, that she knew there was something wrong. 'Is it Lindsey?' I shook my head. I didn't know how to explain what I had been told.

Each time I had to repeat the words, 'Callum has died', it was no easier than the first. Knowing his life was wilfully taken from him made it even more painful. Every time the words fought their way up my throat, it was as though, if the words didn't get past my lips, maybe they wouldn't be true. I really wanted all this to be an awful terrible nightmare, and I hoped someone would shake me by the shoulder and I could wake up. Yet the more people I told, the more it sank in; the more heart wrenching it became to pass on the information.

For a long time, we all moved about as if functioning on automatic. It was painful coming across his favourite toy, finding his clothes at the bottom of the laundry basket, or even hearing his favourite song. No matter how sleepy, no matter how moody, and whatever else was going on, Callum would always stop what he was doing to have a dance with Cher. Her song, *Believe*, was his favourite, and he wouldn't listen to us when we said that twenty times in a row was perhaps too much. He would smile knowingly, 'again'. And we'd play it again because we loved seeing his smiling eyes, and watching him dance on his still unsteady legs.

I wanted Cher to know how much joy she had brought into such a short life. I wrote her a letter, telling her what had happened and how much Callum had loved her song. I didn't let Lindsey know at first, because I didn't think it would be fair for anyone to intrude on her grieving process. Once I had received a reply, I felt I should own up.

I was surprised when Cher's letter did arrive (see pages 148-9). I wasn't even sure she would get around to reading my letter; after all, you hear of so many superstars who are far too busy for their fans. So many of them employ people to deal with their correspondence, but not only did I get a reply, it was handwritten, and signed personally. It wasn't one of those standard letters that could have been signed by a secretary. I was touched by the fact that she made the effort to read my letter, and then take the time to write back. Mine must have been one of hundreds that arrived that day.

I wondered what sort of reaction I would get from Lindsey. My biggest fear was that she would be angry. As it turned out, she told me I was right, and that Cher should be told she was making people happy with what she was doing. I felt that song would allow me to have happy memories of a wonderful child.

The letter, along with Callum's favourite song, kept us strong, and we were better able to cope with our emotions after all that had happened. Even now, Cher's song *Believe* is, for me at least, the right combination. The rhythm is bright enough to get me on my feet just as quickly as Callum did, and the words now have a more poignant meaning.

We decided after the funeral to transfer the fish he had loved so much into a pond. So we set about planning it, drawing and sketching on every scrap of paper until we all agreed on how it should look. Even before he could walk, Callum would speed across the room on his hands and knees, trying to see the fish in the tank. Any time anyone mentioned fish, even in the context of food, he would crawl at high speed and point to the tank. We thought it was a fitting tribute.

For Helen's fortieth birthday I thought I should get her the Border collie she had always been after. I never expected it would ease her pain, but I'd hoped it would make her a little happier. It had already been named Fly. Helen decided it was a stupid name, and then almost at the same time, we remembered it was the name of one of the songs played at Callum's funeral. Because of the association, I don't think either of us are willing to hear Celine Dion's song again. It is a moving song, and for us it seems to be the essence of what we felt when we heard it at the church. Anyway, we decided to keep the dog because of the name, and he was a wonderful puppy, but soon started to expect more attention than we were able to give, so we later gave him to Brenda.

We all got ourselves into a routine, waiting for the trial. At first we didn't dare allow for even the slightest variation in what we had to do. With time I got used to Callum not being around, but getting used to not seeing him didn't mean it stopped hurting.

I expected to feel something when I heard Plender was convicted and sentenced to life. Yet I felt nothing. I couldn't understand how he could spend his life in prison, safe, warm and fed, while we would have to live with our loss for the rest of our lives. He denied it all to the very moment he was found guilty, so there is little chance he will be released on parole.

People say that time heals. I can't say I can agree completely. The pain never goes away; the pain never becomes any smaller. The shock wears away, and with time, the pain becomes a little more bearable. Every day since, I have woken up, and the first thing I think of is how much I miss that tiny child. I don't miss him any less as time goes by, and it doesn't hurt any less either.

CHER

Dearest Lindsay,
to be able to write something to you
that will in some small way bring
you comfort and lighten your impossibly heavy burden. I'm not sure how to
do this but maybe for this moment
while I write and you read we can
carry it together.

When Sonny died last
year I thought my Heart would break.
I cannot imagine the pain you are
going through. Please know that all
of my prayers, love and energy go
out to you, your parents and Callum.
He sounds like such a loving special
little boy, who made everyone's life
better for having known him, even for a
short time. I did'nt even get to know
him and yet he has made an impact
on my Life. I will keep his memory

148

CHER

in my Heart and when I sing "Believe"
it will be His song. I can't think of a
greater honor than having a pure little
soul love my music. maybe you will
send me a picture of him and I will
put it in my dressing room when I go
out on tour. I will think of How he
loved my music and always try to
sing my best to that He hears it and
is Happy.

I know It is probably the
last thing you want to hear right now
but please try to have faith and "Believe"
and do _something_ with your life that
will make him proud of you!

All My love

maybe this is not my place to say this to you
Lindsey but bitterness will hurt you and

I can't bare to think of you having to
go through that as well. God will Punish
or Karma or whatever you want to call
it.

149

Chapter Sixteen

A T-junction

I HAD not managed to start the recovery from the breakdown when we lost Callum. We were just about getting over the shock of that, only beginning to grieve, and realising that the others around us were going through the same thing. It is so easy to imagine no-one else feels hurt, and it is so easy to get caught up in your own pain that you become unaware of anything and anyone around you.

Then one day, I had the choice, either to allow myself to lose the battle I had been fighting all my life and give up, or fight my way through to victory. Sometimes it is easy to make a choice when the only option is to look forward to a new beginning. I had come to a T-junction in my life, where I was put into a position of knowing I couldn't go the way I had gone thus far, and had to change. I could either head one way, objectively dealing with my past, accepting that it will affect my future but that I was actually in control, or go the other way, into denial, pushing my fears and feelings so far down into the abyss in order to pretend they did not exist.

I was in the car, driving down a long road with humps so frequent that it felt like a tread-mill for sea-sickness sufferers. There was a car coming towards me across the junction I was trying to pass. It was moving faster than I had anticipated on such a road. The other vehicle was on a minor road, and was supposed to give way. Before I had a chance to even consider how to get out of the way and or even to brake, I heard a thump, and the click of the automatic locking system. I noticed it was a woman driving and then the other car had lifted onto two wheels and shot past me. As she hit my car, it spun, changing the direction I was facing, and her car swerved and was stopped by a wall on the opposite corner. I saw a child flung from one side of the back seat to the other, its scream similar to the movement, both like the twang of an elastic band.

I'm in the wardrobe, six years old, scared and in the wardrobe. The air is musty, I can smell him on the other side. He is impatient and angry with me, at the same time excited. I don't want to get out. I don't want to stay. My breath feels stale in my lungs, as if I have never breathed anything other than the air in the wardrobe.

The doors are locked. I know I am trapped inside. I can see smoke swirling in the air, getting thicker and darker as I watch it. I know I am not safe in the car. It won't be long before the flames start to lap hungrily at the metal of the bonnet, the smoke then settling thick and black on the windscreen.

I'm holding on to the pyjama cord, as if keeping it hidden will keep me safe. I know this isn't even a minor obstacle to him. I can feel him on the other side, trousers around his ankles, one sock stretched and taut around his lower calf, the other crumpled and lifeless. I know he won't pull it up until he's finished.

Someone is knocking on the window, but I can't be sure because it might even be my imagination. I must concentrate on what I need to do. The steering wheel seems heavy and immobile; I must figure how to get past it. I have to think about climbing out.

I'm standing in the bath, the now tepid bubbly water lapping at my ankles. Ison's hand is soapy and roaming over my genitals. I look at the taps and they don't seem as shiny as they were this morning.

I take the seat belt off, and my lungs expand immediately, so I have no choice but to gulp air. At the same time, pain tears at my chest. I need to press where the belt had been to ease the pain. Then I feel a new type of pain. I must not touch my skin; like a bolt of electricity, the pain intensifies with any movement from inside, and any contact or pressure from the outside as well.

The wallpaper with its almost invisible joins, except in that one spot, where Dad's hand had slipped as he tried to line up the pattern. I can see the edge, curling slightly, not yet torn, just stretching and tempting anyone who sees it to pull it away from the wall. I look at it, knowing that however busy I make myself before bedtime, it will not stop him from coming to torture me later.

I crawl over the front seat, trying hard and failing miserably not to have any contact with the things around me. I feel tender all over, and I realise I need to avoid anything that could prolong the situation. I lean against the car, trying to calm my breathing before doing anything else.

I can see the kitchen table set up for breakfast; Brenda is hovering about as she normally does during her morning routine. I wonder how to tell her. I look around. My plate has the tiniest chip on it, as if over-enthusiastic washing up had worn it away. The middle prong on the fork has lifted a little higher than the other two. An ashtray sits at the other end, already half full.

Inside the car, I was scared to be by myself. I felt trapped, and I had to get out into the open. The accident only gave my panic a further sense of urgency. My flashbacks would petrify me, but the car in its current state could be life threatening. Once outside, I feared any human contact. I needed to be cocooned and safe, away from any further harm.

My skin glistens with ice-cold sweat, each and every hair standing to attention as if expecting some shock. Then I see the hot sticky liquid squirt into the air, and everything around me turns black.

The police were there, as were the Nuneaton Fire Brigade, and a film crew. They were accompanying the fire brigade, filming their daily life for one of those reality shows or something similar. I found out later that they, the film crew that is, were hoping someone would be trapped in the car, so they would have something interesting to film. If they had turned up sooner, they may have been in luck, but as it was, they missed it.

The wardrobe closes in on me as if trying to push me out. Perhaps Ison couldn't open the door, but he could because he holds the key. He decides when I go in, and he decides when I go out.

I was approached by a police officer, who needed me to tell him what had happened and, while he was making notes, a paramedic came by to check me over. I told them both I was fine. I was breathalysed and given the all-clear.

I am leaning over the bed and bent at the hips, my elbows on the duvet cover feeling cold. Ison's body is heavy and awkward on my back. He pulls away and something warm and gloopy hits my spine. Immediately he turns from me, and his footsteps get lighter as he leaves the room.

I didn't want to recognise speech directed at me, or anything akin to a touch upon my skin. A paramedic comes over to me, wanting to know if I'm all right. I tell him I'm fine to get home, and that I'm sure I have no real injuries. I tell him again. I think he believes me, or gives up trying to persuade me otherwise. Either way, I head for home.

Clammy fingers grip me, squeezing and sliding; my whole body shudders with disgust, he thinks I like it. Ison nudges me to move into a position more suitable for him to continue what he is doing. Fear and revulsion freeze my muscles, and only my brain screams at me to get away.

I don't want unnecessary contact with anyone. I want to escape him. I don't want to have to deal with any complications now. I'm now scared because anything could be a trigger. I can admit the flashbacks scare me, maybe even more than the memory of the actual abuse.

The cold droplets of sweat trickle down my spine. Ison's hand is on my shoulder as he leans in to kiss me. I shudder with revulsion. His hand moves from my shoulder and down my arm; too soon, he will prise my legs open. I see nothing in front of me; I'm just staring into the middle distance. Suddenly I see a comic under the other bed, the thin paper, the pages curling from regular and frequent reading, and the once bright inks smudging and blending one into the other.

I start walking and, at every step, fear seizes at my heart, clenching it, squeezing the very life source out of it. I push my way forward, knowing once I'm behind my own closed door, I will be safe.

I see his face, his eyes greedily staring at me, his features flat, almost nondescript, his little eyes just a touch too close to each other. I hear his voice syrupy as he's talking to Brenda, demanding and threatening to me. When he gets what he wants, his voice trails off dismissively.

I open the door, and rush through to sit on the edge of the sofa, wrapping my arms around my knees. I should be safe. I am away from harm, yet the images from my memory flash before me, like photographs or slides.

For a while, with every blink, the image changes, each one worse than the last.

Blink: Lying in the dark, Ian asleep, footsteps by the door. The sweat pours out of me.

Blink: The drawer filling up with chocolate, each one a bribe.

Blink: The coal fire heats the room, my pyjamas hanging in front of it.

Blink: a small white plastic hairbrush, the bristles squashed flat in Ison's hand.

Blink: the tip of my nose pressing into the back of my hand as I push him away.

Blink: his black trousers, slightly hugging across the hips, shiny from the iron either side of the seam.

Blink: the duvet lifts up and away from my hip, my genitals pull themselves back against my body as if I can provide them the protection they seek.

Blink: two naked bodies, two men lying head to toe across my bed.

Blink: my hair sticks to my forehead with sweat. I try to sleep, knowing Ison will be back.

I sit there, waiting for this feeling of suffocation to leave me. I grow impatient as it soon becomes clear that I need to concentrate hard to escape this smothering fear. The heavy weight on my chest is real and imagined at the same time. I dare to open my shirt and check for damage.

Lying on my stomach, I try to lift my head, to turn it this way and that, I'm trying to uncover my face so I can breathe as he lies on top of me, his whole weight seemingly on my chest. He lifts me by my hips, flipping me over, as if to him I'm weightless. I cringe; all I can see is his smarmy grin in the darkness.

I have to consider my options. It is difficult to imagine anyone would listen to me when my own mother ignored me. I can remember also things being mentioned in passing to doctors, who just dismissed it as attention seeking. It was my fault, I was unruly. It was my fault, I was making up stories. It was my fault I should have kept quiet.

I can see the cracks in the pavement as I walk along, slowly filling with dust and rubbish, but still distinguishable from the slabs. Brenda's shoes stop clacking against the concrete, and I know what is coming. She is about to tell me not to mention ever again what I had told her.

I try to stop the image from playing before she opens her mouth, but there is nothing I can do to block out the sound of her voice.

No! Damn it! It wasn't my fault. I know that as soon I was able to, I put a stop to it. I told my mother, because I thought, I expected her to stop something I wasn't able to. I had never forgotten what had happened; I just kept quiet about it because everyone around me had persuaded me to do so. But now, after the car crash, when it all returned to play over and over again before my eyes, I realised I couldn't keep quiet any longer.

I didn't know where to start. Who could I turn to? The last thing I wanted was to be told by the police I had left it far too long for them to be able to do anything about it. Now that I'd had the courage, and I was ready to deal with it, I didn't want to risk any knock backs.

I knew Helen was going to be supportive, whatever was about to happen. I decided to see what sort of help was on offer. I called all the organisations on the list of numbers my counsellor had given me. It was a long, daunting list. It was tiring just to look at it. I had never realised there were so many people offering help to someone like me. I never thought to ask if there was anyone willing to do anything for those in my situation.

The first thing though, was to see a doctor. As the adrenalin began to wear off, the physical pain became more intense, and it was becoming more and more difficult to ignore. I had whiplash affecting my neck and shoulders. I had torn the ligaments across my sternum. The ribs I had broken previously, or I should say had broken for me, had impacted, the shattered edges turning inward.

I had a thick red and angry mark running diagonally across my chest from where the seatbelt had lain. Had I been going any faster it would have been deeper in my skin, tearing at it until it became a puss-oozing welt. Just a larger version of the sort of marks Bob used to leave as souvenirs then.

The doctor had decided to refer me to a counsellor, and to be honest I was a bit dubious. I couldn't see myself sitting in a chair talking about myself for an hour a week, with someone just looking at me and making 'there, there' noises for the duration.

It did, and it didn't, match my expectations. That first session was a conversation where I actually felt I was on an equal footing. She had warned me that counselling could never be considered an easy ride. It was not something to take on lightly, but the rewards were often so much more than what was expected. Once we started talking about me, I felt like a caged animal. I was defensive, trying to determine my right to feel the way I do. It took me a little while to realise that was never going to be taken away from me. Another thing I had not realised was that counsellors are there to support; they will not fight your corner, but they graciously allow you to deal with things in your own time and fashion.

In the beginning, it felt like I was going to a torturer who would re-open my wounds once a week and pour salt into them until it was time for me to leave. After the first few sessions, I began to realise I could mention an instance from my past, without having to relive it, or having to relive the emotion that was intrinsically a part of it. So many times, I would spend half the session or more, just lost in thought, something akin to daydreaming. Talking is not important, but what is said, and isn't said, is. I have never been made to feel I was under any pressure to do anything, except keep the appointments.

I can't remember how many times I had been before I could mention

Ison by name, and then be able to finish the sentence without having a flashback. I was given a list of several pages with names of charities and organisations that may be able to help me.

One by one, each door would open a little, in fact just enough for it to be slammed in my face. One organisation only dealt with women who had suffered at the hands of men. I was made to feel as if I was meant to be despised. Being a man, I couldn't possibly understand what real suffering was like. I decided to ignore all those on the list that seemed extremist.

Others were more sympathetic, but unable to offer any real help. Most suggested I get in touch with a counsellor, and an embarrassed silence followed the sudden attack of throat clearing when I told them that was how I got their number in the first place.

I got in touch with an organisation called ROSA, because they offer help and support to male victims of rape. I asked them if they dealt with systematic abuse as well, and they told me it didn't matter if it happened just once or several times. It was still traumatic to wade through the system, in trying to get heard. They were aware that the hardest part of any form of sexual abuse is actually having the courage to report it, and then to go through with the process that follows.

I was given yet another list of agencies and other bodies willing to help people in my situation. I was now sure I had reached a T-junction in my life. I had the choice of either doing something about it, with the help of the authorities, by trying to get the guilty punished, as I had been all these years, or I could try by myself to push my feelings deep down inside, hoping I could avoid them for the rest of my life. I knew I was no longer willing to carry on ignoring the consequences of what had happened to me as a child.

I was terrified as to how the police would react. Would they believe me? Had I left it too late? Would I have to write the statement out for myself? Would they be looking for ulterior motives as to why I would choose to make my statement now? Would they ask why my mother never brought me in as soon as I had told her? Would they question me, interrogate me, if I couldn't remember exactly what they needed to know? Would it be me sitting there, terrified of giving the wrong information, feeling I was being judged instead of Ison?

The guys at ROSA offered to accompany me at the interview, and it was nice to know I would have their support, but the police preferred for me to speak to them by myself. What surprised me was that they were willing to come to me, to do the interview at my house. I found out later that they train their own officers in dealing with statements such as mine, and the reactions it could cause in the person having to give evidence. They had seen that most people react better when they are in a known environment. I sat down, and a young DC sat also, with a notebook and a pen at the ready. She smiled sweetly, and explained I had nothing to fear; if something didn't make sense, she would ask questions and I would be able to read it all through before signing it.

I didn't know where to start. I wanted to blurt out that he had ruined my life. But I knew she would need details. I wanted to do this properly. I was worried about the sort of language I could use, and I thought hard about the sorts of words that would be acceptable in describing some awful acts. I was also worried that if it was too detailed I would cross the line so that it would become graphic? Apart from anything else, I wanted to make sure that after all this time I didn't make any mistakes. I didn't want to be responsible for something putting a stop to me seeing Ison convicted and sentenced for what he had inflicted on me.

The DC told me to start with my name, address, and date of birth. Then the taking of the statement was mostly a question and answer session. What happened the first time? Who was around? When did it happen? How can I be sure? As I answered those few questions, I began to see how the information needed to be presented. I was starting to understand which details make a case solid, and what is just a matter of interest. I manage to keep my story to the bare minimum of fact. There was no need for detailed explanation of emotions and fears. The whole point of it was to give as much information about what had happened in as little space as possible.

My statement went on for thirty pages, the longest on such a subject in the county's recorded history of similar cases. It was explained to me later that most statements made at the time of abuse are not detailed because they are given by children. Adults who give statements are often fearful about making mistakes because of the time span between the abuse and the writing of the statement. Although I hated them, I had to be grateful I had such clear flashbacks, with realistic images, rather than just a sense of fear or an overwhelming sensation of emotion. This meant I was able to describe in great and accurate detail what had happened.

There was one detail that was obviously missing from all of this - dates. I was scared to pinpoint any incident to a particular date because I could never be sure I had remembered it correctly. I was often truant, so every day of the week was like any other. I could remember winter being different from summer, but as I had spent most of my life trying to block it all from my memory, the days blended into weeks, the weeks into months, until it became one tangled mess of images and emotions that I didn't want to know about.

The questions put to me were helpful, because they would ask, 'how can I be sure such and such an incident happened then?' As an example, I was able to say with certainty that one incident occurred in 1977 because I can remember the Queen's Jubilee and the street party. Summers are obviously easier to remember because all the other children were on their school holidays, and I can remember playing in a larger group. And also the fair would come to town. It was something that was discussed by the kids at great length. Other strong associations would be, snow, Christmas, Easter eggs, Palm Sunday, with all the crosses placed all through the fields, and the little ones hanging by the front doors.

I found it difficult sitting still for the duration; it was as if I didn't want to hear what I had to say. I didn't want to have to relive my experiences, and I'm sure there were several periods of silence where I said nothing at all, just waiting for the last image before my eyes to fade, and leave a moment to consider what I should be saying next. But I found the patience shown by the officer taking the statement reassuring. I knew I was finally being listened to. I knew someone was going to at least attempt to do something about it.

I was told they would keep me informed. I was given a crime reference number, and if I had any questions relating to the case, they would be able to assist me best if I used that reference in any correspondence, or when calling. What would happen next was also explained in great detail. They would keep in touch along every step of the way, and I would be reassured that something will be done.

That same night, once I managed to get to sleep, I started dreaming. I could hear a cackle, a big raucous laugh, satisfied and triumphant. It took me some time to realise it was me.

Now I would just have to wait for the case to come to court.

Chapter Seventeen

Keresley in Context

IT MAY seem quite confusing, but there are actually three Keresleys in quite a small area. A place name ending in 'ley' usually denotes a clearing in a wood or similar. It comes from the Saxon term *'leah'*, meaning clearing. The first part of the name may be a mutation of a word for watercress, which probably grew in the area, as it still does.

As kids, we used to wander through the fields, and when we got bored we would find a patch of watercress and stop to have a nibble. Most people in the area believe it may be a derivation of a personal name. There seems nothing conclusive to prove either. Whichever it is, the fact that there are three of them, means that the people who were deciding on place names weren't very imaginative.

The one thing about metal detecting, that I love so much, is that I never have to go very far from where I live in order to find something fascinating from history. Like an onion, our history shows in the ground as layer upon layer of different times. In more or less the same spot, it is possible to find proof of life throughout the ages. There is evidence of all those different influences that have created our country and culture into what it is today.

I rather enjoy this practical study of history, and I love to be able to learn about the place where my personal history started. The village of Keresley End has a long history. Although not mentioned in the Domesday Books, the first written record of it is in mid-twelfth century when the Lord of the Manor at the time granted a part of the estate to Coventry Priory. This seems to have been a common practice, especially for those with a heavy conscience. By the fourteenth century, it was recorded that there was a population of about one hundred and fifty people, and most of them were, in effect, tied to the manor.

Once the Tudors came to power, feelings of guilt were literally flung out of the window, as Henry VIII, in particular, seized church property to fund his spending habits. One such piece of land was on the boundary of Radford and Keresley, where the present Tamworth Road lies. This road was changed at one point from public footpath to private road, and a toll was charged for the use of it. This didn't seem to last very long, and it has to be assumed that it wasn't very practical to implement the toll, so it soon became a public highway. By the twentieth century, of course, it was to be a major road.

It is now also an estate of sorts, but providing housing for the masses rather than for only one or two families. The original estate was owned and run in succession by several families who all seem to have met an untimely end. There are rumours of murder and people disappearing in mysterious circumstances. It was known as a site that went back as far as about 1410. When it was a Benedictine priory, the Tudors confiscated it, and during the sixteenth century, a mansion was built there, becoming a fine residence suitable for an Elizabethan gentleman.

The industrial revolution was a time when the village bloomed. Most of the villagers were farmers, yet some were weavers providing for the Coventry cloth trade. The original settlement was at Keresley Green, and a new settlement grew at Keresley Heath towards the end of the eighteenth century. In 1852, the church-run school was first opened, and functioned successfully until it closed in 1944.

In 1911, the village was about to take on what was to become its most recognisable image, when a coal company sunk shafts nearby. The company didn't start to operate for another six years. The actual settlement around the colliery was named Keresley Newland. What would later become known as affordable housing was provided for all the workers, and a social club was formed and given a home in 1924.

Five years later, in 1929, Keresley Hall was converted into a convalescent hospital, and in 1942 it was incorporated into the Coventry and Warwickshire Hospital. Its busiest period was during the Second World War, when the majority of patients were soldiers coming in from the hospitals at and near the front lines. It finally closed in 1968.

Mining, and any work within the coal industry, was a low pay, high labour combination. It was hard and dirty work, and it was mostly unappreciated. Most workers would also keep livestock and/or grow their own vegetable patch. The houses may not have been big but they were not the common or garden two up, two down seen in most parts of the country. One luxury was provided though, and that was inside toilets. This was most unusual at the time, especially for the manual labour force.

The RAF volunteer reserve placed its HQ at Keresley Grange in 1937. About ten years later it became a children's home. At the beginning of the Second World War, the colliery was producing up to one million tons of coal a year. 1947 saw the nationalisation of all the collieries, and this brought an influx of workers from Wales, and from further afield in Britain. Then a little later, from abroad, including places like Eastern Europe. This was a time of great growth and change. A year later, Condon Hall became a hotel. In 1950, Newlands House became an old people's home. We used to play in its shadows, as it was, and is still, more or less behind the house Ian and I grew up in.

1964 was an important year, because it saw the opening of the Golden Eagle Pub, and also the library in Bennets Road. I don't know when it all started, or how long it will go on for, but the actual village seems to float over the boundaries of Bedworth and Nuneaton with Coventry. I used to think no-one knew where the actual border lay. I'm sure it used to move at the convenience of one council or another, because I can remember we used to receive letters from both at the exact same address.

It didn't really affect our everyday life, not that I noticed at least, but things would get complicated if we wanted to change schools or dentists. We would be told we were in the wrong catchment area for something, and a while later we could go ahead and make the change because we were in the right catchment area.

Sometime during the seventies, there was a house fire where three children died as a result of it, and then there was the abduction of Julie Stiles from one of the fields I used to play on. These two images stand out in my memory of Keresley because they were such rare occurrences. It seemed to me a genuine calm and peaceful rural place to live. I just happened to be growing up in a house that was the exception that proved the rule.

At the time of the miners' strike, I was resting at her Majesty's pleasure, so I didn't get to see the riots and the demonstrations in the village, or throughout the country for that matter. In places where the majority of people rely on something that is likely to be taken away from them, they will do anything necessary to preserve what they already have.

The mindset of the country at the time was, 'a job is for life', but with the pit closures, it became blatantly obvious that that was no longer the way to expect things to happen. I guess I was one of the first generation who had to realise that change is the key to success. We all had to learn to adapt, and do it quickly. I suppose I was lucky in that I never settled into one job, nor would have been happy to. But what happened in the mid-eighties was understandable for that time and that way of thinking. It has been said that miners came in from outside during the demonstrations and the riots to make more of a statement. There were even burnt-out cars, and stories of looting.

I did wonder if I would have taken advantage of the situation to vent my anger and frustrations, but I think I would have found it too cumbersome having to get involved in someone else's fight. Bob was one of the few who couldn't care less about worker solidarity, and he worked through all the strikes.

There were probably days when he barged past the picket lines, defiant and defensive, but, most often, he would have gone slinking in through a side-door. It could be said that he was just trying to maintain an income to provide for his family, but in some families, where there were members who were on opposite sides about the question of strikes, there were huge rifts, with some families still bearing grudges even today.

It closed briefly in 1991, that is with only a skeleton workforce running, and re-opened fully in 1994, but it finally closed for good in 1996. The Dawmill Colliery nearby is still running, and managing the workload taken over from Keresley Colliery. The Honefire plant, with its distinctive hexagonal-shaped coal, stayed open till 2000. It was quickly replaced by a business park which also flourished.

By the time I got around to deciding on the photographs for the book, the pit was already well and truly gone from the landscape. I had to struggle to find a photograph. I suppose it isn't the most beautiful of scenes, and it can't have been the sort of thing people wanted to look at, especially when they worked there.

I know exactly where it used to be, because I used to look at it every single day while I was living in Keresley. Someone visiting the area wouldn't now be able to recognise where it used to be on the horizon, and even my memory plays tricks on me, when more and more often I find myself struggling to remember where it was exactly.

So that pretty much describes where I lived and the sort of place it is. I could joke that it would need to borrow a horse to become a one-horse town, but it is still most certainly a village, partly due to growing in the greenbelt, and partly because of the mentality of the people. I like the fact that it is a village; the community seems closer than in the towns.

Since I started trying to put my thoughts down on paper, I have, in some way, managed to understand what I've been going through. Having to explain it to someone else invariably gives you the opportunity to make sense of it all. It is as if helping someone else understand, is a sort of cleansing process.

It has been a painful process, and there were days when I hated myself for starting it in the first place, because I just wasn't able to express what I was feeling. The scars from long ago seemed to open up, becoming fresh wounds that I couldn't possibly imagine would ever heal again. Yet knowing there are people who would want to read my story, and knowing there are people who could gain something from reading it, gave me the strength to carry on.

Although thankfully rare, my story isn't unique. This sort of thing happens, and is happening to many. It is still a taboo subject, even though more and more people are aware of its existence. Because this is something that is not talked about, children do not feel able to volunteer any information. When they do, they need to be heard, and, more importantly, they need to be listened to.

While I was writing my story, many things changed, some good, some bad, but all in all, nothing so disastrous as to put an end to my life. It may sound like a simplified philosophy, but no matter what happens in your life, the sun will still rise in the east the following morning. I do not believe in fate, and with my life experiences I've had no proof that when things are bad something or someone steps in to make everything right.

I am maybe a little envious of people who do think like that, because maybe they don't worry as much. I seem to have spent most of my life trying to escape. After all that running I found I was still as close to my life as I had always been. I realise now it is about taking control, making decisions, and accepting the consequences.

I have since had some contact with Justin, and in the beginning, I realise now, I was trying just a little too hard to please him, as if that could make up for the time we lost away from each other. We got together more or less at Nada's insistence; it seems Justin was getting a bit much for her to handle, so she wanted me to step in. I didn't think that was fair to either Justin or me, so I told her I would see how it goes.

At first we were both uncomfortable. After all, we should be close. A father-son relationship is a natural one that should take very little effort, yet it was more of a struggle than I had anticipated. Justin came with all these pre-conceived ideas about me; why I had left, and why I didn't get in touch. He also seemed defensive, almost as if he believed I was going to step in and take over everything.

I was beginning to see a very different picture of myself, not just through my son's eyes, but also how he had interpreted his mother's view to create an image of me. It wasn't a pretty sight. There was a possibility of reconciliation, but it wasn't long before I was under the impression that I was being used. Justin would come to me, telling me how badly I treated his mother, and how callous I had been by ignoring him when he was growing up. I tried to explain, but he didn't seem interested. His idea of a solution was for me to buy his love. I find it hard to believe a fifteen-year-old would decide something like that without any influence from those closest to him.

I was disappointed. I wanted to be a father to my child, not an open bank account. I wasn't willing to allow my son to treat me that way, nor to have him think it was an acceptable way to treat anyone. However angry I get, I will always love him, and I can only hope that he will be able to learn something useful from me.

Perhaps one day Justin will realise there are two sides to every story, and that he never gave himself a chance to hear mine. I didn't want to be used because I was willing to provide for him. I wanted us to get to know each other so we could one day be the father and son I had intended from the moment I found out he was on his way into the world.

I know that I am beginning to heal, but I do not feel ready to risk being mistreated, especially not by someone who has in effect only just come into my life. I am still too fragile to knowingly walk into another negative relationship. Unfortunately I think I should do what is probably going to be the hardest thing I have ever had to do, and that is walk away.

I may not be a good father, but I seem to be doing better at being a grandfather. Lindsey's son Morgan is a great comfort to me. Although we can't help but compare him to Callum, we can already see he is a very different person. As I sit at the computer to write, he thuds up the stairs, pushes his way into my lap, and tells me. 'Okay Granddad, we can start now.' What amazes me is how quickly he learns, or more to the point, how slow I am. The two of us would be sitting by the computer, and his mother would tell me how to do something, and by the third time, both Morgan and Lindsey are exasperated. He then starts telling me what I need to do. He is a friendly, sharing child, when he is visiting, and when we go to see him, Morgan always insists that we eat together.

At the age of six, when I was trying to stop the abuse myself, I did what came naturally, first I said no, and then I tried physically to put a stop to it. That didn't work, so I sought help. When my mother dismissed my comments, I realised I would have to do something myself. I can still remember the fear I felt, because it all seemed so hopeless. I hated myself for not being able to do anything. I also hated the fact that no-one else wanted to do anything about it.

It was painful, being rejected and turned away at every door I came to. There are so many organisations offering help, though none are tailor-made. It took me a long time to realise that no-one has all the answers, and I have to find them by myself. All the organisations offer support, but for the most part, healing old wounds is something you have to do by yourself. But one thing I have to say is, had I given up on asking for help, asking to be heard, I would have imploded with rage.

I once heard a saying about still waters wearing rocks away, and it may be just the right analogy for this book. Persistence is the key, and even if you move forward with the tiniest of steps, you must remember that you are still moving forward. Life is a one-way road, there is no going back. It can't be changed, as I realised, but it has to be understood, and learned from. I never wanted to go through the sort of life that was forced upon me, but I have managed to grow as a person from my experiences. I have managed also to recognise that what doesn't kill you makes you stronger.

I cannot allow anyone, not even the closest members of my family to do anything that would delay my healing process. I can't be sure that, with the sort of life I have lived, what will follow can ever be normal. I realise, I imagine, that I will never be able to wipe the slate clean.

I'm not sure I will be able to describe what I am feeling now. It seems to be an awful combination of emotions. I can describe how each individual feeling affects me, but it is all distorted by everything else that is happening and has happened before. I know I loved my mother, and I suppose I still love the mother I had up until she turned me away, up until the moment her love for Bob was more important than her love for me. I hate the fact that soon after my mother's rejection, my father also disappeared from my life. The vacuum that his leaving created dragged Bob into my life.

These are all things I had no control over, and which have affected me most of all. I was a small child who believed help would be given if I asked for it. I still believe that, and have tried not to turn anyone away when they have come to me. The other thing absolutely out of my control was the sexual abuse I was forced to endure. It has taken me a long time to recognise that I may have been a victim then, but I no longer need to be a victim now. It is possible to get out of that role, but it is difficult and painful, although I know that making that decision was as good as being halfway cured.

That may seem a little drastic, because I know I will never be rid of my past. No-one can cure a past, and I know trauma is not something that can be cured, but there are always ways to make life with it a little more tolerable. It is just a matter of searching long enough to find the most suitable.

This story and, in turn, my whole life, has been about belief. I always believed there was a way out, and when I turned to others and no help was offered, I had to believe I could find my way out by myself. Now all I have to do is accept what happened and try to live with it.

I have to learn to believe in myself.

Chapter Eighteen

The Sentence

ON REFLECTION, it took me a little time to realise what I had done. I didn't know I had it in me; I never knew I was capable of such strength. As the police officers walked away from my house that afternoon, I felt a little taller and a little prouder. I was also sad that I hadn't been able to do it any earlier.

Still, it was a nice feeling to know I had made the choice, and followed it through. I was able to say that I no longer cared what other people thought about me, or what had happened to me. I had taken control, and set the ball rolling.

Hayley, the police officer who had dealt with my statement so delicately, got in touch with me, telling me she was going to keep me informed of what was going on in the case. She explained they had found Ison at his last known address, and that he had been brought in for questioning. He was then arrested, with nine charges being brought against him.

No-one was able to tell me what he had said in the interview, or how he had behaved, but, from the conversation, it was possible to pick up subtle hints, without being told anything directly. I had the feeling that they had reason to be confident.

We had almost daily contact with the police. They would call, or even come to visit me at home, trying to reassure me that things were moving as they should. It was difficult to judge how the case would continue, because being an historical case, it was rather difficult to prove. Most, if not all, physical evidence has disappeared. Any bodily damage would have recovered over the years. All they had to rely on was my memory. Many similar cases had fallen by the wayside because information could not be corroborated. When it comes to the crunch, it could be pretty much my word against his.

I understood, all too well, how much easier it would have been had the police been able to see physical evidence of what I was saying. I had to think objectively, and make myself realise that other people can't see the damage that he's done. Skin heals, bruises fade, lips do not leave traces to be seen by others, although everything that he had done was indelibly marked in my mind.

It was during one of those conversations, that Hayley let it slip that Ison had said something along the lines of, 'whatever *those boys* have said. I did it.' I suppose, subconciously, I knew, but it was something we never talked about, although, in passing, Ian had made his feelings clear whenever Ison was mentioned. It still came as a shock to hear the police and Ison talk of us and *those boys*. It confirmed what I had known all along, but I had not wanted to admit it.

It also made my fears more real. I had often wondered if he had gone on to do the same to others. I knew he had children and, with a violent shudder, I couldn't help wondering why. There were hints thrown into conversations that there were others who would come forward with statements. If I were to regret anything in my life, it would be not having the courage to speak up before. Some nights I lay awake feeling guilty because I knew he may have put other kids through the same abuse.

I tried talking to Ian about it, and the most I could get from him was an admission that he had given a statement. I can only assume he had been put through the same violations, because he refused to say anything other than how much he hates him for what he did.

I was pleased that he had admitted what he had done, and that the case could progress. Then, almost in the same instant, I was plagued by thoughts of him getting away with it still. Would he flee the country? Would he attempt suicide? That scared me most of all. That would never be justice, because it would mean he had both abused me, and taken his own life at his choosing. I felt sick, knowing that option was still open to him. I hoped Ison wasn't having the same sorts of thoughts.

After giving my statement in mid-February of 2003, I was told it wouldn't be very long before the case was prepared for trial. It took about seven, maybe eight, months before the case was ready to go before the Magistrates. I was finally allowed to sense that something was being done.

Obviously, I wasn't allowed anywhere near him or the court while the court was in session. I had even been warned that I could jeopardise the case if I did see him, or, more to the point, if he saw me. It had happened once before; I went to an antiques fair, held in a church in Nuneaton, on Tuesdays and Fridays. I was there with my mate John, looking for something or other; it became immaterial when I saw him. Ison stood there, holding two cups of tea, exactly as he was when I was a kid.

Short, scrawny, with his almost featureless face; the most memorable thing about him are his glasses. He made eye contact, and he must have recognised me, because in the moment I turned to John to tell him I wanted to speak to someone, he had disappeared. I searched for him, sure that, even in a crowded place like this, I would spot him. I ran outside, looking this way and that, searching for those glasses, expecting to see his hairline at the height of others' shoulders.

He was just as smarmy as he had always been. I suppose, in his head, he thought he would appear slick and confident. All I could see was how slimy he was, his need for gratification oozing out of every pore. He functions for one thing, and one thing only. In that moment when I noticed him, I knew he had done nothing in his life except to try to attain his sick and perverted pleasure.

I knew I couldn't do anything about it myself, and, with the way things were dragging on, there were moments when I wished I could just leave him hanging from the lamp-post outside my window, so I could watch him dangle and rot. Or my other favourite one, is a big blunt and rusty knife, and everyone, who has reason to, helps dice him into one-inch cubes.

That moment passes, and I realise now it is perfectly natural for me to have such feelings. They are justified, but I also know that the best way to deal with things is to tow the legal line. Taking the law into your hands, means you have to be responsible for your actions, and I want him to answer for his actions. The whole idea of it is not for me to get justice, but for the state to protect me from injustice. I kept quiet at the time, so they didn't know anything had happened. Now that I had told them, and they were willing to do something about it, I wasn't going to let my personal feelings get in the way.

According to the law, under the Sexual Offences (amendment) Acts 1976, and 1992, a victim of a sexual offence is entitled to anonymity throughout his or her lifetime. This obviously restricts how the court can function, and how the case is to be reported, as I found out to my painful frustration. From the very first hearing, it was all to happen behind closed doors.

When I found out he was going to go to court, I was led to believe that he would be putting forward his pleas to the charges against him. I couldn't be there so I was tempted to get a relative to go instead, to sit in the public gallery. It wasn't worth the risk. The time since that first incident with Ison was so painful, it kept playing on my mind. I knew it needed closure. I wasn't expecting the pain to end, just to feel a little relief at knowing he would be punished for what he had done.

I wanted to know every detail of what went on in the court. Who said what; how did Ison behave; what did he say; how did he say it; did he look guilty? My questions were endless, each one desparately needing an answer.

It was frustrating and painful; anyone who had been there was listening to cases of no importance to me, watching how sometimes stupid mistakes were affecting the life, and often lives, of those involved. But, at the end of the day, I still had no confirmation that Ison had turned up. Had Hayley lied to me? Did he escape? Could he not be bothered to show up? Is he still treating my pain and fear as a big meaningless joke?

I couldn't spend the whole day just sitting on my hands; I called Hayley several times during the day, trying to find out what had been going on. I wanted to know what would happen next. Had he been abrupt and dismissive, telling them I had given them a pack of lies? Did he stand there, eyes focused on his shoes, head too heavy with shame to look anyone in the eye, his guilt permeating through his insolence?

At a quarter to five that Tuesday afternoon, I finally found out from Hayley that Ison had been before the court at eight-thirty in the morning. The matter had been adjourned for a fortnight. She explained to me that the case was presented to a closed court because of Ison's safety. There were also other issues that needed to be dealt with, anonymity being one of them. If justice was to be done, I knew, deep down, that they needed to keep him safe and alive; he needed to have his say. It wasn't clear if the next hearing would be before a closed court.

A very brief piece appeared in the local newspaper, so a journalist covering the court cases had managed to find out what had gone on, because Ison was mentioned by name. There was nothing more in there except his name and that the case was going to be adjourned for pleas and directions, and the nine charges were all to do with sexual abuse of local boys from the 1970s. I was annoyed that he wasn't pressed into giving a plea, because it was slowing things down.

Depending on the pleas, the case would either go to trial, or straight to sentencing. Either way, the case was going to be transfered to a Crown Court, because the type of charges were likely to receive heavier sentences than the magistrates could issue.

I heard later that he had been harrassed; he was fearing for his life, or playing for time. The Crown Prosecution Service was telling me they had a strong case, because of the taped admission, so they decided to move him. Whoever was doing the chasing, obviously got wind of it, and found him again. The police said, from then on, that there would be no point in trying to move him any more, because they couldn't guarantee he wouldn't be found again. It was probably safer for him to be where he is now.

I have to say I wasn't very tempted to go after him. No, really. After so many years, I have learnt how to keep myself and my temper under control, and I am insisting on seeing things done properly. I knew he hadn't strayed too far from the village, so, if I had wanted to, I could have done something to him, but I think I wanted him to know, to realise, that what he had done isn't just objectionable to me, the whole of society abhors his actions. The only way to show him that, would be in a court of law.

It was one adjournment after another. It was dragging on much longer than I had expected, but Hayley kept telling me it was perfectly normal for things to go like this. I hate the fact that it is all behind closed doors. I hate the fact that he gets special treament. I have to sit at home, waiting for Hayley to ring to tell me what is going on. While Ison, on the other hand, sits in an office in the courthouse, drinking tea, munching on biscuits, getting the treatment of a welcome visitor instead of being treated with the contempt he deserves. I have to admit I admire all those people who have any dealings with him, who can keep calm, and talk to him as if he is a normal human being. Innocent until proven guilty; I really admire those who can respect that.

It was becoming obvious that Ison was just stalling for time. I was to find out later that, during a closed court session, he told them that he could admit to the charges, but he couldn't possibly agree to the time as to when it happened. It must be taken into account that he too was a child, and the sentencing must show that.

When I found out, I became blind with fury, and demented with anger. If he were to be sentenced as a juvenile, he would be given a community order, something trivial compared to what I had suffered, and what I was going to be suffering for the rest of my life.

There had to be some proof that we could both be placed in the village of Keresley End at the same time, and up to the end of the abuse. Someone mentioned the Census, completed every ten years, listing where everyone was at the time. I was disheartened to find out that the complete details do not get published until a century after its completion. The relevant questionnaire was completed in 1971, and I suppose the information in the 1981 census could also prove useful, but I wouldn't be given access, and neither would the police. It stays under lock and key, no exceptions.

The utility companies don't keep records of customers for more than five years, unless they're current. Of course, Brenda changed suppliers, so no proof there. The information I needed was thirty to forty years old. The was no point in going to the local council, when the house we were living in was actually provided by the colliery.

A non-existent company does not keep any records. Because the pit finally shut only a little while ago, I did believe there may be someone around who still kept the physical paperwork safe. The question was, was there anyone willing to search through, checking for a tenancy in the name of Chester.

There was no such thing as Council Tax back then, so that wasn't an option of proof of address. I thought of the school register, but, with my attendance record, it was quite likely it would come to nothing. I found out subsequently that schools only keep records for three years after a child leaves or transfers. Time wasn't on my side. I couldn't remember if either Ian or I had library cards. It didn't seem like the sort of thing Brenda would ever have done.

In the end, I remembered something similar to an electoral roll had been taken in Keresley End. It was a registration of all the residents, and they were listed for something or other. I mentioned it to Hayley, who checked it out, and it nailed him. We had, that is to say the police had, written proof, an official record, placing Ison at the age of eighteen and over, in the same neighbourhood as where I had been residing with my mother.

The defence was struggling, but, with this new evidence, they asked for another adjournment, and it was allowed. The case would be put off for another fortnight. The CPS wasn't particularly worried; they knew it was just a formality. In order for the defence to be able to present their case, they would need to look over all evidence presented.

To me, it was a painful torture. There was nothing in the local papers. Without Hayley, it was as if I had ceased to exist, as if there was nothing happening. I was sleeping even less than before; the nights just dragging on, the hours never ending. My fears and flashbacks were playing over and over, stuck on a loop. Fourteen painfully long days passed, and the weather was as shabby as my mood.

I was edgy and frustrated; everything was a nuisance. And to top it all off, my one worthy indoor distraction of the computer and the internet was infested with viruses. I tried to kill time metal-detecting, but, more often than not, I would find myself thinking about the computer and how it was utterly useless until the viruses could be cleared. It reminded me of me. It was exactly how I felt, not knowing, and having to rely on others for information. My computer was manifesting the symptoms I was feeling but managing to hide from the outside world.

That Tuesday, when it finally came around, the day was probably a normal one for everyone else. I can't be sure if it is possible to feel elated and down at the same time, but I wouldn't know how else to describe it. This was the day, after some thirty years, that I was going to find out if there was to be any relief from my never-ending anguish.

A total of fifteen charges were put to him; starting with the most serious, there were three of gross indecency. I was told later that the magistrates wanted the full charges read out, giving the exact details of date, time, and a brief description of the incident in question. Yet it was Ison's lawyer who stood up to say something along the lines of, 'the case needs to go to Crown, so there is no point in going over the details.' I was given the impression that the man had tried his best in difficult circumstances, but he was aware there was nothing for him to do except follow usual procedure.

The court room was full of journalists, and it was quite likely that the case would be reported nationally. I had an appointment with my counsellor, and had to make my way into town to meet with her. The town was buzzing; it seemed there was something going on.

Perhaps it was just my imagination and my expectation, knowing he would be in court and backed into a corner. There was talk of camera crews outside the courthouse, but no-one seemed to know why. Could there have been another case more interesting than Ison? Anything was posssible, and, after all, I was far too subjective about what was happening to me to consider anyone else.

I didn't try to find out. It was difficult not to sneak a peek at what all the fuss was about, and I knew it would be in the papers the next morning. There was also Hayley who would let me know what was going on. On my way back, I planned to make myself a cup of tea, call Hayley, find out what had happened, and then sit down to write.

Most emotions change from how they are at the time, to how you feel about them at the time of writing. I wanted to be able to describe the frustration, the restriction, the anger and, most of all, the awful feeling of jittery nervous energy that shudders through every muscle, that by the end of the day exhaustion hits, even though I have done nothing much.

It was bad news. The case had been adjourned for the afternoon because the magistrates were busy with another case. I thought even a punch in the face would have been easier to handle. The little control I had been allowed in all this, by giving the statement in the first place, was slipping from me because other things were going on.

The afternoon dragged on. There was nothing on the television worth watching; I thought a distraction might help. The computer was infested yet again. One virus was coming in via e-mail, and another through the downloading of pop music. As soon as we found out, we called someone in to put a stop to it, but, as we were already begining to believe, there was no guarantee it wouldn't happen again.

When it finally rang, the noise scared me, making me jump. Hayley was on the phone telling me how Ison had stood there, hunched, almost folding in on himself; he was shaking as the charges were put to him but he didn't say a word. It was his representative who told the court there would be an entry of a guilty plea to all fifteen charges.

I was over the moon. The case was to be adjourned until the 19th of March for sentencing. The irony of it was that Ison was going to be sentenced in the same court that Ian and I were sent down from, along with thirteen of our mates. Sitting in the public gallery, looking down on the chairs placed in the dock, I had a feeling it would have been easier for me to deal with being in the dock, than watching Ison there.

Everyone involved in the cases listed for court two were obliged to be there for the start of the day, and most people were milling around long before ten-thirty. With Helen close to me the whole time, it was a comfort knowing I had her support. A photographer from the Sun newpaper stood there at the ready, waiting for me to point Ison out to her.

We were just chatting, hoping that the more or less mindless banter would camouflage our real feelings. Ian was trying to come up with one one-liner after another, but I could tell this was more of a strain for him than his jokes would lead us to believe. All of a sudden, a green-hooded jacket barges through the group, splitting us in two. He looks me straight in the eye, and recognises me. 'Fuck off,' he said; the first words I had heard from him for thirty years. I assumed it was directed at me, but the photographer shrugged as if to say, 'I'm used to it.' 'Click' went the camera, and Helen smiled at me, trying to reassure me. I knew everything was going to be all right.

He shuffled his way across the court's stone floor; his thick-soled shoes seeming almost too heavy for him to lift. His bright white sports socks peer out from under his light blue pinstripe trousers. The sort of wishy-washy faded colour you would expect a harmless old man to wear. The pr exercise in image made me feel sick.

Seeing him so close to me, all the hatred and fear and repulsion returned, as if what he did had happened just moments before. I felt as helpless and insecure as the child I was at the time. However unrealistic, I felt if he were to make an attempt at physical contact, I was sure I would be frozen to the spot through fear and disgust. It took a moment to realise that I am not a child any longer, and I have the courage to put a stop to the damage he has done to me.

Looking at him as a grown-up, I can see a small and slight, weak man trying hard to peer through his metal-rimmed glasses. I know that there is nothing he can do to me now, yet the sickening thought in all of this is that I am only safe because I am no longer a child. Now that I'm grown up, he only fears me. I realise I have the power to hurt him; I just have to be patient and strong.

I climbed the steep and rickety staircase up to the public gallery of court two, and tried to find where I would be most comfortable sitting. Looking down onto the actual courtroom, I could see it was a sombre and imposing place with a dark and possibly harsh atmosphere. All the green leather writing tables seem well cared for and well worn. I looked at the bench, with the three oversized chairs and their big red leather cushions, and I tried to imagine who would sit there, who would be making today's decision. It was all too easy to imagine myself in that huge chair in the middle, my elbows resting on the edge of the bench, my lips curling into a smile as I wait for silence before declaring the sentence.

No matter where I looked, he seemed to be in my line of vision. He would shuffle around, as if trying to keep an eye on us, and several times while he was in earshot, I heard him singing. I tried not to think that he may be doing it on purpose, that he may be trying to prove how good a law-abiding citizen he is now.

I found myself sitting more or less above the dock, and I could feel the nausea creeping up on me as I realised I would be no more than six feet away from him. The only other feeling I could sense was a frustrating fear. Not a fear that my story wouldn't be heard, that part of the process was over and done with, but the fear stemming from anticipation for what is about to happen.

I try to settle on the cushion in the public gallery, but I can't get comfortable. I try to stifle a giggle when the phrase 'ants in your pants' springs to mind, because I am suddenly aware of the fact that I'm fidgetting more than usual.

The judge dealing with all matters in court two on the 19th of March, is the Rt. Hon. Judge Hodson. I have been told he is a fair man. A heavy rain is pounding against the windows. High winds howl around the building, creating a cold and frightening atmosphere. As the rain starts to fall in sheets, the noise from outside seems to be in competition with the conversations inside the courtroom.

The public gallery is not busy, and as they wait for the first defendant of the day to come in, I notice the graffitti around me, the usual scratchy initials and dates, and very little else. There are also several chips in the wood, where shoes have rubbed at the same point over and over again. The first case is about a burglary committed under the influence of alchohol. A combination of a valuable car and threatening behaviour, brought about a sentence of twelve months. I could only hope the day would go on as it had started.

A case of arson which involved reckless endangering of others, as well as the killing of a dog, led to the defendant being put away for five years and five months. Listening to the details of that case made me feel a little sick. Not because I wasn't capable of hearing those details, but because I realised my childhood will also be discussed in such detail.

Next, a case similar to Ison's. I heard the name and realised immediately it was someone else, yet I had to double-check I didn't recognise the face. A round and bland, almost featureless face, metal-rimmed glasses. The green-hooded jacket placed so carefully on the spare chair. I watched him shake, one hand on the other turning over and over as the details were read out.

'...brought before the court for sentencing... following a confession ... eight counts of making and having indecent photographs of children.' Sixteen hundred and seventy of level one, and two hundred and six at level four, which, it was explained, had included images of penetrative sex. The whole time, he was shuddering more than he was shaking, probably from a mixture of fear and embarrassment as the judge tried to sum up what he had heard. The pre-sentence report recomended a community sentence, a type of rehabilitation order.

The defence tried to argue that the defendant suffered from an obsessive compulsive disorder which meant he had to collect things, and had done so throughout the forty-nine years of his life. The defendant's excuse seemed to be that he came across the images by accident, and was so disgusted that he would download them so no-one else could see them. This was declared to be irrational, which of course fitted in with the disorder, yet no-one was willing to accept there was nothing sexual in his doing so.

The images were collected over a period of three to four years, and there were periods when he would search the sites perhaps once a day. He blamed alchohol for what he did, claiming that he never once found it arousing or stimulating, but in time he began to crave more bizarre images than those he had already seen.

While the court was looking at sample images taken from the two computers that were seized at the time of arrest, we had to leave the gallery. Straight in front of me, as I stood by the door to the court, sat Ison. I noticed him quite by chance. I was trying to work out what was going to happen to the case I was watching. I felt that so much would depend on the sentence for the man with the pictures. I felt that it would be easy for the judge to compare images and actual hands-on abuse.

He was told to stand up, and I watched him as he tried to support himself against the guard rail of the dock, his hands writhing one inside the other, speeding up as we all heard the sentence – eight months custodial sentence, half of which is to be served in prison, the other half on licence.

An interesting fact about the licence is that it is normally only the length of half the sentence, but Judge Hodson extended the licence for two and a half years.

So when we went to lunch, we were all quite hopeful about what we could expect. Before he was called in, I caught the end of another case, but I wasn't really listening to the details; I was far too upset. By this point in the afternoon, I just wanted it to be over.

As I walked up to the door for the public gallery, I saw that he was sitting in the exact same place he was before we left. I had to wonder if he was trying to intrude on our personal space. I walked up the staircase, trying to ignore the fact that he was looking up behind me. It felt as if it would never end, and it was much like being trapped in one of those hamster wheels; there seems no way to stop, and the view in front or, in this case, below me, is terrifying.

My stomach twists and turns, each nerve ending in my body screaming its distress as I watch him enter the dock. I look down; my feet seem to be slipping from under me, and I feel as if I'm standing at the top of a cliff, the drop pulling me over.

The case for the prosecution was short and, to be perfectly honest, pathetic. There were ten charges, six of indecent assault and four of gross indecency. Sample charges showing the sort of behaviour Ison was willing to admit to during the years of 1971 to 1974.

The defence of course, was another matter. We were told that, after going into voluntary care, Ison was caught up in mutual masturbation with a carer while he was between the ages of twelve and fourteen. He was confused. He was experimenting. He didn't understand his emotions. He got into a heterosexual relationship which is still current, so he is married with children, and has the full support of his wife and family.

The breath stopped in my throat, as I saw character references being handed over to the judge. His wife, his son, and his GP, wrote saying what a wonderful, normal guy he is. I shuddered to think what they would consider abnormal. I suppose that, although to me he is an abuser, I can only hope that to them he is just a husband and father.

There was talk of how he works with the elderly, and has been caring for his brother, which he could no longer do because of this matter. He has also had no contact with his grandchild since April.

The pre-sentence report, or PSR, shows Ison to be a man whose past has come back to haunt him. I got the impression that for him it was all a rather embarrassing inconvenience. Never mind my destroyed childhood, he was just a confused youngster experimenting with his feelings. Me having to suffer crippling flashbacks for the rest of my life was a stroll in the park compared to the fact that he was forced to move because his neighbourhood found out what he had done. I swallowed back the tears and the laughter; the irony of it was that he was being presented as the one suffering in all of this. I felt as if I was just a trivial mistake, something that needs to be dealt with as soon as possible.

I had to tell myself that, however bad this was, it surely has to be easier than having to go to trial, having all the minute details discussed for hours on end. I couldn't be sure I would be able to listen to him talk about it, nor could I speak about it myself. And anyway, it was just the summing up to hear, and then it will all be over.

The Rt. Hon. Judge Hodson, sat up straight in his chair, looked at his notes, and I thought I heard him sigh. He tucked both his fists into opposite cuffs of his robe; the silence seemed to be deafening. I can't imagine I have ever been so excited and frightened, so accepting and so defenceless all at the same time.

'It is a difficult case,' he began, *'and complicated by the amount of time that has passed since it all happened. Most cases of this age are dismissed for lack of evidence. Most people accused of such crimes from so long ago, get away with it by saying it is a case of mistaken identity, it just didn't happen, but it must be taken into account that you* (Ison), *admitted what happened at the earliest opportunity, and are willing to take responsibilty for what you did.*

'A man of general good character, with minor...' he stopped and looked at some notes. I assumed he was reading his criminal record; the end of that sentence drifted off unheard. It seemed odd to me that in all the other cases that I saw today, for everyone who had a record, the type of offence was mentioned.

'The sort of sentence I can give is of the sort that would have been available to a judge who was on the bench at the time these offences were committed. It has to be taken into account that you were a young man, and you cannot be punished with the full power of the law just because you are now an adult.'

He talked some more along those lines, but I couldn't hear him properly because I had the sensation of being winded. All that effort we put in trying to prove he continued to abuse me and my brother, even after he had turned eighteen. The prosecution mentioned that the sample counts had happened to me at the ages of six, eight, and nine. With Ison being ten years older than me, this proves the court is incapable of doing simple mathematics, or something else is going on.

'As there is no mention of buggery or anal rape...' and again the fury exploded in my brain, creating the sensation of nothing. No sound, no vision, no touch, just a vile taste creeping up into my mouth. I wanted to scream at them to read my statement, to buy a calculator, but I knew I had to keep quiet.

And so it went on, like white noise, completely incomprehensible to me. I heard the sentence, a community rehabilitation order to last three years. It seemed to me as if the words had been thrown in at random, just to catch me off guard. It came up somewhere in between the Judge mentioning that being abused can't be a sufficient excuse, because neither I nor my brother had gone on to abuse others, but then again Ison is not the man he used to be.

I think I mumbled something about it being a load of whitewash, but I can't be sure if anyone heard me. If they did, the court chose to ignore my outburst and storming out.

I knew if I was going to take in another breath, I would have to get outside. I stood leaning against the cool stone facade; the sandy taupe wall a comfort in its calm exterior. The anger drained from me, leaving me empty and hollow.

Helen came out to tell me Ison had been told he can't work with children under the age of eighteen, not paid or voluntary. Hot and angry tears streamed down her face; I could see she was frustrated at not being able to do anything. I had no tears. I had no energy. I had nothing.

I stood outside waiting for the others. Ian disappeared, and I thought maybe that was a good thing. His wife, Kay, and Helen were talking just far enough away that I couldn't hear what they were saying.

At that moment, as I watched the two women with their arms around each other, I hated Ison even more. He had no right to hurt the woman I love; there was no reason for his actions to affect her.

I knew we should move away from the main entrance, because I didn't want to see him. Well, I did, but I just didn't trust myself not to do anything stupid. We started walking away, and I kept turning back to try to see him slinking away. There was no sign of him. I had to assume he was going to creep out of the back door.

So there he would be, this day and the next, walking the streets with the same right as any other man. His past behind him, a new day in front. He will be able to forget me and the sordid piece of his past that he hoped would never come back to haunt him.

That is unless he reads The Sun. Or meets anyone else who may know him. All I can hope is that, for at least a little while, he will know how it feels not to be able to escape from his past, or from himself.

Somehow, I don't think we've heard the last of Ison...

RoSA

Rape or Sexual Abuse
Support Project

HELPLINE 01788 551151

RoSA is a registered charity dedicated to supporting men, women and young people who have experienced rape or sexual abuse at any time in their lives.

We offer individual and group support for survivors, their families, friends and partners.

Please contact us for more information.

Office: 01788 551150
email: rosa.support@btconnect.com